"What a wonderful and inspiring work; it was a pleasure to read it."

—Alfred H. White, Ph.D., Author of *In Search of Truth*

"I welcomed the opportunity to read this very interesting, informative collection of truly fascinating accounts, validated with details that arouse emotions of every kind. Impressive examples of endurance, determination, conflict, all supported with real moments in experiences that invite very thoughtful reflection of the past, the present and the future. The drama of each brief encounter is strengthened with historic names, places and consequences that those of us following might give thought to as we face our own time with respect for those who came before us and those who will follow us before the return of our Savior."

—Ardeth G. Kapp, Author of *Eyes to See: Recognizing the Lessons in Our Lives* and *Better Than You Think You Are*

MARAUDERS, MISFITS, AND MORMONS

MARAUDERS, MISFITS, AND MORMONS

TRUE STORIES OF EARLY UTAH

GEORGE HUBBARD

Cover Design by Kyson A. Barlow

Original Map of Wagon Routes in Utah Territory from the Library of Congress, Geography and Map Division, https://www.loc.gov/item/2012586633/

ISBN: 978-1-7358338-3-5

CONTENTS

PREFACE

My mind frequently goes back to that Sunday in August 1951 when I attended my first church service of The Church of Jesus Christ of Latter-day Saints. It was in a small branch in Junction City, Kansas, and the attendees were mostly young military families serving during the Korean Conflict.

My wife wore her finest, which included hat and white gloves. She was the only woman so attired. I kept wondering when they were going to pass the collection plate. They never did. Various people would hand small envelopes to someone sitting in front. I assumed they were invitations to something.

As the meeting progressed, different people would go to the rostrum and say something. Then after a song and a prayer, half of the congregation got up and left the room. Those of us who were left had another song and prayer. Instead of a preacher delivering a sermon, a young fellow led a discussion with participation from the congregation. Although I don't remember what was said, I do remember that I enjoyed hearing a lot of scriptures quoted along with their intended meanings.

Then another song and prayer, and those who had left earlier came back. The poor missionaries who brought us tried to explain what was happening. It was all very different from anything I had previously experienced.

As my wife and I continued attending each Sunday and as we listened to the testimonies they expressed, we began to realize that this was not just another religion. This was not just another church. This was a whole new culture. It wasn't just a Sunday thing for those who were there. It was their whole life. They were living, to the best of their abilities, the "good life," and they were experiencing joy and happiness in so doing. I wanted what they had.

After my wife and I were baptized, I developed a two-prong insatiable curiosity to know more about the Church. Through the scriptures and prayerful contemplation, I studied their theology. And through stories I studied their marvelous culture.

My intent for this volume is to present a selection of my favorite stories that will give an enjoyable glimpse into that special culture that we frequently call "Mormonism." The stories are selected for their human interest quality. They are true stories. They are well documented, but many come from sources not usually found in the libraries of most LDS families. Therefore it is expected that most readers will be encountering many of these stories for the first time.

These stories should be interesting to members of The Church of Jesus Christ of Latter-day Saints as well as to non-members. I hope they will be enjoyable to all.

George U. Hubbard

PART I: MEMORABLE EXPERIENCES

REBECCA WINTERS – MAY SHE REST IN PEACE

*I*f you have never heard of Rebecca Winters, you are in the majority. Her name does not appear in many history books, and what fame she has did not come until after her death.

Rebecca Burdick Winters was one of the several thousand Mormon pioneers who set out from Winter Quarters, Nebraska, bound for their promised land in the valley of the Great Salt Lake. But Rebecca never made it to her intended destination.

Rebecca, along with her husband and five children, embarked from Winter Quarters in 1852 as members of the James C. Snow party. While following the North Platte River in western Nebraska, cholera struck the travelers, and Rebecca nursed and cared for many of the sick -- until contracting the disease herself. She died on August 15, 1852.

After wrapping the body in blankets, Rebecca's family buried her in a grave just east of present-day Scott's Bluff, Nebraska. Her husband, Hiram, insisted that the grave be deep enough for protection from wild animals, and boards were placed on top of the body for further protection. A family friend, William

Reynolds, obtained the steel rim of a wagon wheel, and he spent much of the night chiseling the words, "Rebecca Winters - Aug 1852 - Age 50," into the rim. William's five year old daughter, Ellis Reynolds, held candles while her father did the engraving. They then propped the engraved rim in an upright position to mark the head of Rebecca's grave.

For about 40 years the grave was just another of the thousands of graves that marked the Mormon and Oregon trails. Then in 1892, as the Chicago, Burlington, and Quincy Railroad was building westward across that part of Nebraska, Rebecca received the fame that had awaited her. The railroad's planned right-of-way would place its tracks exactly on top of her grave.

At this point, the story diverges into two versions. The more romantic version is that the railroad officials, upon discovering the grave on their proposed right-of-way, voluntarily chose to resurvey the route in that area and reroute the tracks in order not to disturb the grave of this "honored pioneer." The other version of the story is that Norman DeMott, who had homesteaded the land, sold it to the railroad with the stipulation that the grave not be disturbed, and he spent a great amount of time legally forcing the railroad to honor his stipulation. At any rate, the right-of-way was resurveyed, the location of the tracks was changed, and Rebecca Winters' grave remained undisturbed. The tracks, when laid, were six feet away.

Later developments are that many of Rebecca's descendants gathered at her grave site in 1902 and erected a stone monument. In 1929, the local chapter of the Daughters of the American Revolution placed a bronze plaque at the grave site, and they assumed responsibility for maintaining the site. But because of the danger of visitors meandering too close to the mainline railroad, the Church and the railroad agreed in 1994 that the grave should be relocated. It is now 15 feet from the tracks and about 900 feet east of its original location. In its new location,

Rebecca Winters' grave site still attracts hundreds of visitors each year.

As a result of the railroad's decision to build around rather than over the grave, Rebecca Burdick Winters has become an icon and a symbol of the courage and perseverance of the thousands of determined pioneers who moved America westward in spite of overwhelming hardship.

～

References:

Will Bagley, *The Salt Lake Tribune*, July 15, 2001.

The Rebecca Winters Story, National Park Service, U.S. Department of the Interior.

Historical Marker 21, Scottsbluff Chamber of Commerce, Historic Land Mark Council.

BRIGHAM YOUNG GETS A LESSON IN RAFTING

Generally speaking, Brigham Young's word was law. And in retrospect, he was usually right. There were, however, occasional exceptions to this rule, and one exception occurred in 1847 when Young's party of Utah bound pioneers reached a point on the Platte River where they had to ferry their wagons across.

Calling the group together, Young explained how he wanted the raft built.

"It will not work," Thomas Grover responded.

"I think it will," Young replied.

Thomas, relying on years of prior experience with rivers and boating, said more resolutely, "It won't work in this kind of stream."

He then retired for the night, but before he could go to sleep, one of the men in the group questioned him about his views.

"I have forgotten more about water than Brigham Young will ever know," Thomas claimed. The man went immediately to Brigham Young and told him what Thomas had just said.

The next morning, Brigham Young called Thomas Grover to task. "Did you say what I am told you said?"

"Yes I did," Grover answered. "I was raised on the water and don't know anything else. When the raft strikes the current, it will go under."

The raft was constructed according to Young's specifications, and with a wagon on it, it was launched. It floated well at first, but when it reached the rapid flow of water, it capsized and the wagon and its contents were lost.

Turning to Grover, Young said, "My plan failed. What is yours?"

A new raft was built, this time to Grover's specifications. Working all night at the task, the men had it ready to launch the next morning.

Grover ordered, "Put the heaviest wagon on it."

Protesting, Young said, "Shouldn't we try it with the lightest wagon?"

"No, I want the heaviest." And so it was done.

With its heavy load, the raft left the river bank, and when it hit the heavy flow of current, it continued safely and reached the opposite bank without incident.

After getting all the wagons safely across, Young appointed Thomas Grover to stay and be in charge of ferry operations for other companies of pioneers who were on their way. Thomas and a support crew remained at that post until the water in the river subsided enough so that further ferrying was not needed. Back in good graces, he then came on to the Salt Lake Valley and rejoined his family.

~

Reference:

Joel P. Grover, *The Ancestry and Genealogy of Thomas Grover.*

THE DONNER PARTY LEAVES A VITAL LEGACY

One of the epic tragedies in America's westward movement occurred in 1846 when the Donner Party became trapped in the snow while trying to cross the Sierra Nevada Mountains into California. Only one day from the summit, a heavy snowstorm halted their progress and resulted in a frozen isolation leading to starvation and death of several party members along with a degree of cannibalism by survivors.

Bound for California, the Donner Party was given a choice between two possible routes after reaching Fort Laramie (in present-day Wyoming). An established route led northwest along the Oregon Trail to Fort Hall (in present-day Idaho), then westward, and then along the Humboldt River to a crossing point of the Sierra Nevada. But an explorer, Lansford W. Hastings urged the Donner Party leaders to take a short cut leading to Fort Bridger, then over and through the Wasatch Mountains, along the southern shore of the Great Salt Lake, and through the desert to the same crossing point into California.

Choosing the short cut, the Donner Party found the Wasatch Mountains to be almost impassable. To get through with their wagons, they had to cut trees, remove boulders, and hew wider passages through narrow corridors of granite. Fortunately, they had the necessary equipment, but their progress was extremely slow. From present-day Henefer in Utah, the 30 mile trek through and over the mountains into the Salt Lake Valley was a 30 day ordeal. The trail they blazed is the legacy that they left.

The following year, in 1847, Brigham Young and the pioneers followed the same route as the Donner Party. But because they traveled a route that had already been blazed and cleared by the Donners a year earlier, Brigham Young's advance party received the gift of time. Even though the Saints had to do some additional cutting and clearing themselves, their trek through and over the Wasatch Mountains took only four days instead of the 30 days required by the Donner Party.

In commenting on the Donner Party's legacy to the Saints, George Albert Smith, eighth president of The Church of Jesus Christ of Latter-day Saints wrote:

> But for the success of the well-equipped Donner Party blazing a road from Henefer over the mountains to the valley of the Great Salt Lake in 1846, consuming thirty days, the Mormon Pioneers who came over the same trail a year later in only four days could not have reached the Valley until too late to plant their crops and preserve their seed, particularly potatoes.

Lest it be thought very unfair and cruel that the Donners should suffer such a tragic fate in the Sierras after leaving such an invaluable legacy for the Mormons, it should be pointed out that because of disorganization and squabbles within their own ranks, the Donners lost several more days of time after entering the Salt Lake Valley. Had these internal problems not occurred, they would have reached the Sierras in ample time for safe passage into California.

~

References:

Walter M. Stookey, *Fatal Decision* (Salt Lake City: Deseret Book Company, 1950).

C. F. McGlashan, *The History of the Donner Party* (Stanford: Stanford University Press, 1954).

ADVICE FROM ABRAHAM LINCOLN

here was really nothing special about Andrew Jackson
Stewart, and yet he had some interesting experiences.
A convert to The Church of Jesus Christ of Latter-day Saints,
Jackson, as he was known, lived with his widowed mother and six
siblings in Beardstown, Illinois, while the city of Nauvoo was at
its height.

When ten or twelve years old, Jackson was nearby when a
young girl, Eunice Haws, was playing by an old well. Without
realizing the potential danger, Eunice moved too close to the
edge of the well, and the ground started caving in beneath her. In
an instant, Jackson dashed to the well, and rescued Eunice just as
she was about to fall in. When Eunice's mother learned what had
happened, she gratefully told Jackson, "When she is grown, you
may have her for a wife." The two children grew into adulthood,
and they indeed did become husband and wife.

As a young man, Jackson earned money hauling passengers
from Beardstown to the train depot in nearby Springfield. On
one occasion, he carried some men who were going to work on
the railroad near Springfield. For unknown reasons, the men

refused to pay for their transportation, and even though Jackson still had their trunks, his efforts to collect his fares were unavailing. As a last resort, he sought legal counsel from Abraham Lincoln. Feeling that the case was not worth legal proceedings, Lincoln gave Jackson some effective advice.

"Take their luggage, Mr. Stewart, you already have it, and pawn it for the amount due you, and then if those gentlemen want their trunks, they may redeem them."

As soon as the men learned of what Jackson had been advised to do, they came forward, paid their fares, and redeemed their trunks.

In May 1850, at the age of twenty-nine, Andrew Jackson and Eunice Stewart joined a group of Saints migrating to Utah, arriving after a four-month trek. A month later Brigham Young called Jackson and Eunice, along with two other families, to settle an area where Payson, Utah, is now located. Jackson became clerk of the new Payson Branch. A monument now commemorates the spot where they planted their first crop.

~

Reference:

Kate B. Carter, *Heartthrobs of the West* (Salt Lake City: The Daughters of the Utah Pioneers, 1932).

HOW TO GET A GOOD DAM BUILT

*W*ater is essential to man's existence, and it was especially vital for establishing the LDS colonies in the Great Basin. Besides having water for drinking, cooking, washing, and bathing, the pioneers also needed it for watering crops and livestock and for turning mill wheels.

In the settlement of Cache Valley in northern Utah, a small group of pioneers attempted to form the settlement of Weston on Weston Creek between Clarkston and Oxford. Arriving at that destination in 1865, they stayed a year and then abandoned it because of Indian uprisings, but they returned permanently in 1869.

Upon their return the settlers immediately set to work building a dam across Weston Creek. They attempted to install a framework of willows in the stream. They improvised racks of small willows woven to hold dirt, which they used to carry load after load of rocks and dirt to the dam site.

It was a slow and difficult project. After working all day, the men would sleep at night and then return to the job the next morning only to find some of the previous day's work washed away. It was a very discouraging operation. They might not get water to their planted fields in time for the growing season

Then one morning when the men returned to the job, they were surprised to find that not only was the prior day's work still there, but additional logs and mud had been applied. Although pleased, they were mystified. How had it happened? And then they understood.

The beavers in the stream had finally gotten the idea that a dam was to be erected, and they had joined the work force. They cut willows into the appropriate lengths, wove them into the framework, and daubed them with mud. Thus with the men working the day shift and the beavers working the night shift, the dam was completed in short order. And it was a very good dam. In only four weeks, the settlers had water flowing in their irrigation ditches, and their grain was off to a good start.

~

Reference:

Joel E. Ricks, "The Settlement of Cache Valley," *Utah Historical Quarterly*, Vol. XXIV, No. 4, October, 1956, pp-319-337.

SAM HOUSTON SPEAKS OUT ABOUT
THE UTAH WAR

In 1857, President James Buchanan ordered the U. S. Army to march to the Territory of Utah to quell a supposed insurrection of the Mormons in the newly organized territory. Now what, if anything, does that episode have to do with Texas? It turned out that Sam Houston, a U.S. Senator from Texas, became one of the most vocal critics of the expedition.

The expedition was initially commanded by General William S. Harney. Becoming needed elsewhere, Harney left the expedition while en route and was replaced by Colonel Albert Sidney Johnston. The expedition then came to be known as Johnston's Army.

Sympathizing somewhat with the Saints' reactions to the inhumane treatment by corrupt and autocratic Federal officials in their territory, Sam Houston decried the sending of the army. In an oration on the U.S. Senate floor, Houston suggested that instead of having sent an army, "why not send them men to whom they could unbosom themselves." He further suggested that if the United States would send "honest men and gentlemen, whose morals, whose wisdom, and whose character, comport with the high station they fill," that the Mormons would likely be willing to surrender to them and act in obedience with the laws of the United States.

Houston was especially incensed by one incident that occurred just outside of Utah. Being bogged down for the winter and running out of supplies, the army was in a state of severe hardship. Salt was especially needed by their cattle. Learning of the situation, Brigham Young sent a large supply of salt out to the army with the message that it was a free gift, but if the commander preferred, he could pay a fair price later. Being loathe to accept anything from the "rebellious Mormons," the Union commander refused to accept the salt at all.

To Houston, refusing the salt, besides being an act of needless discourtesy, meant that if the soldiers had to resort to eating their cattle, the unsalted meat could produce cholera which might be especially fatal to men in tents in such severe winter weather.

Continuing his oration on the Senate floor, Houston said, "What was the message the military officer sent back? I believe the substance of it was that he would have no intercourse with a rebel, and that when they met they would fight. They will fight; and if they fight, he (the commander) will get miserably whipped. That was a time to make peace with Brigham Young, because there is something potent in salt. It is the sacrament of perpetual friendship."

Peaceful arrangements finally prevailed, and Johnston's Army was allowed into the Salt Lake Valley the following Spring without shots being fired. Brigham Young accepted the new Territorial Governor appointee, Alfred Cumming, as an honest and fair-minded man, and the supposed rebellion existed no more. When the U. S. Government policies and actions became consistent with Sam Houston's expressed views, peace and harmony prevailed.

Reference:

Writings of Sam Houston, 1858, in Texas Archives, Austin, Texas.

EMMA LEE WAS ONE FEISTY PIONEER

 Survival on the early frontier required a high degree of perseverance and toughness. Emma Batchelor had those qualities in abundance. And besides that, she was not a lady to be messed with.

Emma, who had no trouble accepting the Saints' early practice of plural marriage, was not shy about letting her desires be known. Following a buggy ride with John D. Lee, who was in Salt Lake City as a delegate to the Territorial Legislature, Emma announced her desire to marry Lee. (NOTE: As nearly as possible, the spelling and punctuation in the quotes to follow are as Lee recorded in his diary.)

> Emma expressed an attachment for me & said that I on first site was the object of her Choice. I replied that I would lay the case before the Gov. (Brigham Young) & obtain his council; & when convenient I would let her Know the result.

After interviewing Emma and determining the sincerity of

her intentions, Brigham Young performed the ceremony and Emma became one of Lee's nineteen wives.

Lee and his families resided in southern Utah where he succeeded in amassing lands and wealth through his industriousness. But in so doing, many other men, not so industrious nor successful, were envious and sought at times to take advantage of him. But when they made the mistake of involving Emma, they soon regretted it.

On one occasion, Emma learned of some letters that had been written accusing Lee of participating in the infamous Mountain Meadows Massacre. Emma figured out who had written the malicious letters, and she lost no time in confronting the men. According to Lee in his diary, Emma accused George Hicks of being "a poor sneaking pusillanimous (sic) Pup & always Meddling with other men's Matters & that he had better sing low & keep out of her Path or she would put a load of salt in his Backside."

Taking offense, Hicks complained to the local bishop who decided that both Emma and Hicks should be re-baptized as a sign of their repentance of such un-Christian-like conduct. Emma accepted the verdict reluctantly but not passively. At her request, the bishop agreed that she could select the person to do the baptizing.

"I am much obliged," she said to the bishop. "I demand Baptism at your hands, seeing that you are so inconsiderate as to require a woman to be immersed when the water is full of snow & Ice & that too for defending the rights of her husband. You should pay a Little of the penalty for making such a decision & perhaps if your back side gets wet in Ice water you will be more careful how you decide again."

The people who were present cheered for Emma and cried out, "Stick him to it, Emma, it is but just." But on the appointed day the bishop had to be in another town on business, and the scheduled baptism never occurred.

References:

Juanita Brooks, *John D. Lee* (Glendale: The Arthur H. Clark Company, 1961).

Juanita Brooks (ed.), *A Mormon Chronicle: The Diaries of John D. Lee* (San Marino: The Huntington Library, 1955).

THE INDIANS HELP PETER SHIRTS
PLOW HIS FIELDS

*P*ioneer life was difficult and perilous on southern
Utah's frontier. It was difficult because of the uncer-
tain success of growing crops in that desert region with its infre-
quent rainfall. Despite the arid conditions, spring floods caused
by the melting snow in the mountains frequently wiped out
hastily constructed dams and sometimes destroyed entire settlements with loss of life to livestock and to humans. The relative
isolation of the settlements from the more settled northern
colonies added to the difficulties.

Life could also be perilous in southern Utah because the Indians, on the verge of starvation each winter, would steal, plunder,
and even murder for food they needed to sustain themselves.
Brigham Young's philosophy toward the Indians was that it was
better to feed them than fight them. This policy worked as long
as food was available to the Indians; and thus the Saints provided
large amounts of food and clothing for the depraved Paiute
Indians of that area. In their missionary zeal, the Saints also
attempted to convert and baptize as many Indians as possible.
Because the baptism of an Indian was usually accompanied by a

gift of a blanket or a shirt, many of the Indians repeatedly showed up each spring to be re-baptized.

The Peter Shirts family settled in this environment, out on the southern Utah desert away from any settlement. With thrift, industry, and plain hard work, they managed to eke out a living sufficient to sustain themselves. To protect themselves from the plundering of hungry Indians, they built a wall around their gardens and living area, and thus they lived inside of a makeshift fort.

One spring after a particularly hard winter, a band of hungry Paiutes came seeking food and clothing. "I will share a little food with you, but I can't give you much. We didn't have much this year." Shirts told them. Although taking what was offered, the still hungry Indians were dissatisfied. Convinced that Shirts was holding out on them, they attacked and tried to force their way into his fort. In the ensuing battle, one of Shirts' two oxen was killed. Even if he and his family survived the attacks, spring plowing would now be impossible.

Somehow, Shirts managed to communicate with the Indians and convince them that since he could not plow and plant seed, no one was going to have enough food that year. "You killed one of my oxen," Shirts told them. "Now we are all going to go hungry." Recognizing the gravity of the situation, the Indians laid down their weapons and agreed to cooperate. They allowed Shirts to hitch six of them to the plow, and thus these same Indians who had been trying to kill Shirts and his family were now pulling his plow and plowing his fields. Dire circumstances on the frontier had turned deadly enemies into cooperating allies.

Reference:

Juanita Brooks, *A Mormon Chronicle: The Diaries of John D. Lee* (San Marino: The Huntington Library, 1955), Vol. 2, pp 255-256.

THE PANGUITCH QUILT WALK

$\mathcal{T}$he Great Quilt Walk from Panguitch to Parowan in southern Utah is one of the more unique episodes of the settlement of the Great Basin area by the LDS pioneers. Although it is without parallel in the annals of LDS pioneer lore, it is a relatively unknown episode that deserves much more attention than it has so far received. It was a desperate, and successful, attempt to obtain relief for the starving settlers of Panguitch during the severe winter of 1864.

As part of Brigham Young's colonizing process, a company of Mormon pioneers from the Salt Lake Valley moved down to southern Utah in 1851 and established the community of Parowan. After having done so, some of these same colonizers moved eastward in 1864 and founded Panguitch (originally known as Fairview). But the Panguitch pioneers, who were in a more isolated location between the Markagunt and Paunsaugunt Plateaus, had a very difficult time getting established.

That first winter in Panguitch was bitterly cold. The snow was deep, and communication between the two settlements had ceased because of the difficulty of travel. The Panguitch settlers had not had a good fall crop, and food supplies were becoming exhausted. As a result, the Panguitch settlers were on the verge of starvation. Relief had to be obtained from neighboring Parowan, but it required that someone travel to Parowan to inform the people there of the desperate situation in Panguitch.

It's only about 40 miles, as the crow flies, from Panguitch to Parowan. But a 40 mile trek by land won't quite get you there. Today's roads go around the mountains that are in between. And taking the direct route by foot or wagon is a challenge for the hardiest of men, especially if the winter snow is on the ground. Although the deep snows and the cold temperature made such a trip seem like an impossibility, it was clear that it had to be attempted by a relief party.

The community leaders in Panguitch organized a relief party to be led by Jesse Lowder, a counselor in the local bishopric. Many of the local men responded to a call for volunteers, and six were selected to accompany Lowder on the desperate and dangerous mission. In addition to Jesse Lowder, the relief party consisted of Thomas Jefferson Adair, Jr.; John Lowe Butler, II; Alexander Matheson; Thomas Morgan Richards; John Paul Smith; and William Talbot. With a wagon pulled by a pair of oxen and with quilts intended for warmth while sleeping, the group set out for Bear Valley, hoping to go from there over the crest of the hills and then down into Parowan.

Every step in the deep snow was a struggle for the rescue missionaries. Upon reaching the head of Bear Valley, they found further wagon travel to be impossible, so abandoning the wagon, they proceeded on by foot. In those areas where the snow was relatively shallow, they made progress, but when encountering the soft and deep snow at the higher altitudes, they sank in up to their hips. It soon became apparent that they could not go any further and that their attempt to obtain relief for their starving community would end in failure. It was now time to plead with the Lord for help.

Spreading a quilt on top of the snow, the seven men knelt in a circle on top of the quilt, and they prayed for the way to be opened for them to complete their mission. As they finished their prayer, they realized that while they were on top of the quilt, they were not sinking into the snow. The answer to their prayer became clear, and they now knew how to proceed. Laying quilts down in front of them, they resumed their trek by walking on the quilts. After walking across one quilt, they laid another down, and then another, and they walked on this moving platform of quilts without sinking into the snow. In this manner, the seven men made their way across areas where the snow was too deep for normal walking, and they succeeded in arriving in Parowan and alerting the people there of the plight of the Panguitch settlers.

The people of Parowan immediately made food and other supplies available. The seven men of the relief party embarked on their homeward journey carrying sacks of flour and other foods, and the citizens of Parowan promised to follow up with further supplies as quickly as possible.

The homeward journey for the relief party was different from their original journey in two respects. In one respect, it was even more difficult because the seven men were now carrying heavy sacks of food supplies. But in another sense, it was an easier journey because the relief party members now knew that the trip could be done. Again, it was their quilts that enabled them to traverse the areas of deep snow and arrive successfully back in Panguitch. This rescue mission has become known in Panguitch as "The Great Quilt Walk."

In his journal, one of the quilt walkers, Alexander Matheson, recorded the following account of the overall experience:

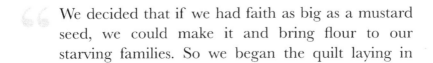

We decided that if we had faith as big as a mustard seed, we could make it and bring flour to our starving families. So we began the quilt laying in prayerful earnestness. The return trip was harder with the weight of the flour, but we finally made it to our wagon and oxen and on home with thankfulness. The whole settlement welcomed us because we had been gone longer than expected. There had been prayers, tears, and fears which turned to rejoicing and cheers.

In memory of the seven-member relief party and of the unusual way in which they made the trip, an annual Quilt Walk Festival is now held on the second weekend of June in Panguitch. It is a gala affair with a parade, quilt displays, quilting classes, and an "all you can eat" pancake breakfast. The highlight of the occasion is a dinner theater in which the story of The Great Quilt Walk is impressively dramatized. They wisely hold the festival in the summer, however, rather than in winter.

References:

Panguitch Quilt Walk Festival Brochures and Dinner Theater.

Historical Marker at Panguitch City Library.

NECESSITIES ARE WHERE YOU
FIND THEM

When a people are persecuted and driven as were the Mormons in New York, Ohio, Missouri, and Illinois, the creation of a protective shield against further occurrences of such episodes is a very natural defense mechanism. Now, having been driven to the Great Basin region, far from their previous persecutors and with every expectation of becoming reestablished economically as well spiritually, it was quite natural for the Saints to exercise due caution in relations with the "gentiles" (as non-Mormons were frequently called) who were also moving into, or traveling through, the Great Basin.

With the completion of the transcontinental railroad and the driving of the golden spike in 1869, towns populated by gentiles sprang up along the route of the railroad in northern Utah. As a general rule, the Saints sought to avoid the "corrupting" influence of the more worldly gentiles as well as wanting to avoid a resumption of persecutions from which they had fled so often. Therefore, the Saints of that era tended to avoid contact with the gentiles.

The new town of Corinne, Utah, near the golden spike site,

was one such gentile community. Located on the main line of the railroad not far from Cache Valley, Corinne and its residents were well stocked with the necessities of life.

On the other hand, because of their relative isolation, LDS settlements in the Cache Valley of northern Utah and southern Idaho were not well stocked at all. In their settlements not more than 10 to 20 miles away from Corinne, the pioneers of Cache Valley, generally speaking, had to improvise or do without many of the "necessities" that make life easier and more bearable.

Trade and contact with the gentiles was discouraged. But in some cases, the pioneers would temporarily set aside the law of obedience, "the first law of Heaven," in order to provide necessities for one's wife and family.

The people of Corinne needed oats and hay which the Saints had. The Saints needed clothing and furniture which were available in Corinne. From one of the Cache Valley settlements, a man named Mr. Frederickson went to Corinne with a wagon load of oats which he sold for forty dollars. He then bought a cook stove and a pair of shoes for his wife. Others quickly followed his example.

In Christen Christensen's pioneer home in Weston, Idaho, Christen's wife had to kneel down on her knees to cook meals in their open fireplace. Christen also went to Corinne and bought a cook stove.

When the Weston bishop called his congregation to repentance for trading with the gentiles, they stoutly defended their actions. Christen said, "I can't say I feel sorry because I feel pretty good, my wife don't have to set on her knees and cook; so she can stand up straight so I feel pretty good."

Reference:

Joel E. Ricks, "The Settlement of Cache Valley," *Utah Historical Quarterly* (October 1956, Vol. XXIV, No. 4).

LIVE UP TO YOUR COMMITMENTS

*I*n 1861 the Western Union Company was working feverishly to build the transcontinental telegraph line that would link the east and west coasts of America. The line was being built in two sections. One section was building westward from St. Joseph, Missouri, and the other section was building eastward from Sacramento, California. The two sections were to meet and connect with one another in Salt Lake City, Utah.

Whenever possible, both sections employed local labor, especially for cutting trees and preparing the telegraph poles. Therefore, when the eastern section reached the Territory of Utah, the contractor hired a group of Mormon men to provide the needed poles.

Time was of the essence, the project needed to be finished before the winter snows set in. The Saints went to work and were exceeding expectations; that is, until they learned that they were being paid substandard wages compared to other people working for the same contractor. They then walked off the job.

In jeopardy of being unduly delayed and not finishing before the winter storms, representatives of the eastern section went into

Salt Lake City and explained their predicament to Brigham Young. Perhaps, they hoped, he could use his influence to get the workers back on the job.

After listening to the telegraph representatives, Young called in some of the disgruntled workers and listened to them. Then he rendered his opinion.

"You agreed to do certain work for a certain amount of pay, and you are being paid that amount. The telegraph company has kept its end of the contract. I expect you to keep your end. You made a commitment, and you should stick to it."

Duly chastened, the workers returned to the job and completed their end of the contract.

The eastern section from St. Joseph reached Salt Lake City on October 18, 1861. The western section from Sacramento arrived six days later on October 24. That evening Western Union president, Horace W. Carpenter, sent the first transcontinental message. Addressed to President Abraham Lincoln, it said, "I announce to you that the telegraph to California has this day been completed. May it be a bond of perpetuity between the states of the Atlantic and those of the Pacific."

References:

"Transcontinental Telegraph, 186" in IEEE History Center Website.

Clarissa Young Spencer and Mabel Harmer, *Brigham Young at Home* (Salt Lake City: Deseret Book Company, 1968).

WHEN BRIGHAM YOUNG'S DAUGHTERS DIMMED THE LIGHT

*I*n governing his large household with a combination of love and authority, Brigham Young had to establish a few "necessary" rules. While encouraging his ten older daughters of dating age to entertain their beaus in the parlor of their home, the Lion House, Brigham insisted that the coal oil lamp in the center of the room not be turned out nor even dimmed. Therefore, when ten daughters and ten young men assembled in the parlor, privacy and a romantic aura had well-defined limits.

Where there is a will, there is always a way. One night when the romancers were assembled, they hit upon a scheme for reducing the lighted condition. Taking books from the book shelves, they built a well around the lamp, and soon the light went only to the ceiling, leaving the rest of the parlor in relative darkness. For a while, everything went well, and the couples were thoroughly enjoying themselves. Then the parlor door slowly opened, and there stood Brigham.

Without a word, Brigham removed the books one by one, and then he said, "The girls will go upstairs to their rooms, and I will say goodnight to the young men."

No one will ever know what Brigham said to the boys. His words were not recorded. But we can safely assume there were never any further attempts to adjust the lighting in the parlor.

~

Reference:

Clarissa Young Spencer and Mabel Harmer, *Brigham Young at Home* (Salt Lake City: Deseret Book Company, 1968).

ETHNIC CULTURES HAD TO BLEND
IN THE EARLY WEST

The early west was an amalgamation of cultures. Migrants from the eastern states were a composite lot from a variety of backgrounds including business and agriculture. Those from the southern states were primarily farmers seeking land and opportunity. Immigrants from Europe and other lands brought their long standing cultural heritages and their diverse languages. A major common element among all these migrants was that they were moving into an environment that was different from anything they had known before.

At first the mixing of cultures produced animosity and contention. However, the mountainous terrain, the immense open spaces, and the frequently harsh weather posed challenges to all and served to bind the people together in the common cause of survival. Intermarriages among the different cultures also provided a coalescing effect. Communities that began with culturally diverse populations eventually became united in purpose and sociability. A case in point is that of Manassa in Colorado's San Luis Valley.

John Morgan, a Mormon missionary to the southern states

led the first group of Mormons into the hamlet of Manassa in 1878. Coming in two groups from Georgia and Alabama, a rather dramatic transition was in store for these converts. Sensing a need to help the newcomers, Brigham Young sent an initial company of eighteen Danish Saints (as they were called) from the area around Manti, Utah, to settle also in Manassa. Additional Danish families followed shortly thereafter. The Danish Saints, under the leadership of Hans Jensen came in the late summer of 1878 to help the southerners, and Jensen, as bishop, came with ecclesiastical authority over both groups.

Under Jensen's direction the two groups worked together and laid out a town according to established Mormon practice with town blocks 34 rods square and lots 17 rods square, making four lots to a block. While the Danish Saints led the planning efforts, the southern Saints made significant contributions by felling trees for houses and a school and by fashioning timber into railroad ties. The Danes, who had been in Utah since before the Civil War, had learned the techniques of dry farming and irrigation, skills now needed by the southerners. Because of their diverse backgrounds, the two groups brought complementary skills to a common endeavor. A disappointing harvest that fall also promoted mutual cooperation as the people subsisted primarily on a diet of rice and beans borrowed from the local Hispanic population.

Although the two groups had to work together to survive, cultural differences began to emerge. Leadership in the local church and its auxiliaries belonged primarily to the Danes and to others who had moved in from Utah. The southerners began to resent being subordinate to the Danes who considered the southerners to be coarse. The southerners, in turn, considered the Danes to be hypocrites.

Language differences also became an issue. As the population began to expand into outlying communities, the Danes conducted church meetings in their own language when they constituted a majority. Soon, the Danes predominated in the outlying communities, while the majority of southerners remained in Manassa.

In an effort to restore harmony and unity, church leaders in Utah sent Silas Smith, a cousin of Mormon founder Joseph Smith, to assume ecclesiastical authority in the San Luis Valley. In appointing two southerners as his counselors, Smith raised the self-respect of the southern faction. Bound by a common religion, the two cultures began working more closely together, but by 1880, many of the Danish Saints had returned to Utah, and the Mormons remaining in the San Luis Valley were mostly of southern stock.

As the years passed, an amalgamation occurred among the remaining San Luis Valley Mormons as they lived together, worked together, and worshipped together.

~

Reference:

Edward R. Crowther, "Southern Saints: Making a Mormon Community in the San Luis Valley," *The San Luis Valley Historian*, Vol. XXXV, No. 3, 2003.

THE GOLDEN SPIKE CEREMONY MET
WITH AN UNEXPECTED DELAY

*O*n May 10, 1869, the Golden Spikes were driven, and the nation was now linked from coast to coast by rail. There was a grand celebration at Promontory, Utah, as Leland Stanford of the Central Pacific and Thomas Durant of the Union Pacific swung their mauls and simultaneously drove two golden spikes into a cross tie of polished laurel. (It is reported that both men missed on their first swings.)

Electrical wiring had been connected to Stanford's silver plated maul and to his spike so that when the maul first touched the spike, an electric signal would be sent over telegraph lines to California and to selected cities in the east. So New York, Chicago, St. Louis, Sacramento, San Francisco, and other cities were notified at the exact moment; and bands played, cannons were fired, and speeches were offered simultaneously across the nation. The only problem was that the ceremony occurred two days later than the expected date of May 8. The delay, while disappointing to those waiting at Promontory, was infuriating to the waiting celebrants in California and in the East. What had gone wrong?

Stanford and his party arrived at Promontory on Friday, May 7, fully expecting the ceremony to take place the next day. But a terse telegram arrived on the 7th from Sidney Dillon, a Union Pacific executive, stating, "Impossible to make connection until Monday noon." No further explanation was available at that time, but the reason is now known.

On May 6, the Union Pacific train pulling Durant's palace car stopped at the Piedmont station in southwestern Wyoming, and it was waylaid by hundreds of angry railroad workers who had not been paid for months. They uncoupled Durant's car from the rest of the train, and when the conductor objected, two of the mob brandished pistols and suggested that the conductor get aboard what was left of his train and move out. The men then pushed Durant's car to a siding and secured it in place with chains. Durant wasn't going to Promontory until the workers got their pay.

Having no other alternative, Durant telegraphed for $80,000, and his palace car remained under guard. Although another train carrying several companies of the Twenty-first U.S. Infantry was due to come through bound for California, Durant chose not to request their intervention, and that train passed through Piedmont without stopping. The soldiers were scheduled to participate in the ceremony at Promontory and then proceed onward.

On Saturday, the 8th, the ransom money arrived along with an engine sent to pull the palace car to its intended destination. Arriving at Echo City, Utah at noon, the Union Pacific engineer parked Durant's parlor car along side of Abraham Lincoln's former private car in which Sidney Dillon was entertaining officers of the Twenty-first Infantry and their wives. One more obstacle still had to be cleared before the Union Pacific officials could proceed on to Promontory. Spring runoff waters in Weber canyon had made the Devil's Gate bridge impassable, and crews worked feverishly to complete needed repairs on Sunday.

Durant and his party finally arrived at Promontory on the morning of Monday, May 10, and the rest is history.

~

Reference:

Michael W, Johnson, "Rendezvous at Promontory: A New Look at the Golden Spike Ceremony," *Utah Historical Quarterly,* Vol. 72, No. 1.

SOMETIMES IT PAYS TO BE LATE

*I*n August 1854, a horde of grasshoppers swarmed the fields in and around Lehi, Utah, devouring everything green. Fortunately, most of the crops had already been harvested, and no appreciable damage was done. But the eggs laid by the grasshoppers hatched the following year before the harvests were in, and the farmers had to contend with a more serious invasion. Because they had been successful in prior years, the farmers planted on a more extensive scale in 1855, and when warm weather came, the infant grasshoppers also came.

The farmers tried everything they could think of to stop the invasion. They dug ditches, filled them with water, and drove the grasshoppers into the ditches. They laid rows of straw and when the grasshoppers covered the straw, they set it afire. They dug holes in the ground, brushed the grasshoppers into the holes, and covered them with earth. Nothing worked; the grasshoppers still came and devoured almost everything. Relief finally came in the middle of June when the grasshoppers developed wings and inexplicably flew away.

The farmers then planted corn and potatoes in their devastated fields, and because the frost and snow arrived late that year, they found success with those crops. But very little grain was produced that year.

Of the small number of successful grain crops that year, one belonged to Sister Canute Peterson. Brother Peterson was away on a church mission, and the responsibility and labor of producing a crop in 1855 fell on Sister Peterson's shoulders. Making furrows with a hoe, she planted an acre of wheat by herself, and being inexperienced in such an endeavor, she was late and she planted the grain deeper than necessary. As a result, it took longer than usual for the wheat shoots to emerge through the soil, and by the time they finally came up, the grasshoppers were gone. Sister Peterson's field was covered with "luxuriant growth."

In the end she harvested sixty bushels of wheat along with sixty bushels of corn and some potatoes as a result of being late and planting too deeply.

∼

Reference:

Hamilton Gardner, *History of Lehi* (Salt Lake City: Deseret News Press, 1913).

THE GHOST OF SALT LAKE CITY'S
RIO GRANDE DEPOT

*A*long with so many other buildings, homes, and places throughout the world, the Denver and Rio Grande station in Salt Lake City has its own ghost. When the train station, which now houses the Utah State Historical Society, was in its hey-day, it was a beehive of activity for travel between California and the East.

The stories in this book are all supposed to be true. If that is the case, then why is a ghost story included? While there may be many doubters of the veracity of this or any ghost story, it is nonetheless true that the story itself exists. It has been written about in books, and it has been featured on local radio and television broadcasts.

The story has several versions. A common version is that several years ago a woman and her fiancé were having a heated argument on the station platform beside one of the tracks. In his fury, the man threw an engagement (or wedding) ring onto the track. Lunging forward to retrieve the ring, the woman, dressed in purple, fell in front of an oncoming train which struck her. She was instantly killed.

There are those who say that the "Purple Lady" is still at the station. Her presence is most often felt in the large and spacious women's rest room. Customers of the Rio Grande Café sometimes sense an eerie feeling when using that facility. On one occasion, a construction crew reported always hearing music coming from that room.

Other phenomena have also been claimed. Security guards from the Utah State Historical Society have heard her footsteps at night, but could find no one when investigating the sounds. Telephones in the State Capitol Building have received calls from the depot elevator phone when no one was in the elevator nor in the building. Dishes have been broken, objects have been moved, and various other phenomena have been reported.

Although the Purple Lady may not exist, it is a fact that her story is still there.

~

References:

Utah State Historical Society, "Haunted Utah."

Kelly Ashkettle, "Utah Ghost Hunters Break on Through to the Other Side," *Salt Lake City Weekly* (www.slweekly.com).

Take-out Menu, Rio Grande Café, Salt Lake City, Utah.

THE MARSHALS ARE COMING! THE MARSHALS ARE COMING!

*G*enesis, Leviticus, and Deuteronomy were brothers. Their Pa, Brother Jones (his first name has been lost), was determined to give Biblical names to his sons, but his wife put her foot down on Exodus. "He'll always be going somewhere," she protested. The family lived on a farm outside of Elsinore in central Utah.

In 1887 when the boys were approaching their teen-age years, their Pa entered into a polygamous relationship, marrying a widow of three years who had a son with the acceptable name of Joshua.

Because Jones, as a polygamist, was now subject to arrest by federal marshals, he dug a pit in the barn and laid a trap door over it. Should the marshals ever come, his plan was to run to the pit and jump in. Joshua's job was to conceal the trap door with a scattering of hay, and Deuteronomy was to whittle on a piece of wood, whistling all the while, until the marshals left. Serving as lookouts, Genesis and Leviticus were to sound the alarm whenever strangers approached. After a few dry runs, the boys knew their roles quite well.

There was a problem in the family, however. Although the two wives got along fine, their children didn't. Joshua, who was older and larger than the three original boys, considered himself their superior. He loved to tease them and play tricks on them. Finally the three boys had had enough of Joshua.

Genesis came up with a plan for revenge. "We'll play Mormons and Marshals," he suggested, "and we'll let Joshua be Pa. We've got a bucket of rotten eggs that we've been saving all summer, and we'll fix it up under the trap door so when Joshua jumps into the pit, the eggs will all drop on him."

Deuteronomy added, "Let's also get some buckets of muck from the barn yard."

When they had everything all set, they called to Joshua, "Want to play Mormons and Marshals?"

"Sure," said Joshua. "I'll be Pa." The boys knew that Joshua would want the leading role.

They all took their positions, and Genesis and Leviticus shouted out the alarm.

"The marshals are coming! The marshals are coming!"

Acting the role of Pa, Joshua started running toward the pit in the barn. But Pa also heard the alarm, and he also started running.

"Git outta my way, son!" Pa yelled to Joshua.

Joshua ducked and Pa dove for the trap door and the pit down below. The boys then heard several plops as the rotten eggs and the barnyard muck dropped on their father. They also heard some bellows of rage from below. That was one problem.

The other problem was that the marshals really were coming. The alarm that had been given was real, not just part of the game. Two strangers arrived at the barn just as Joshua, back in his proper role, finished spreading hay over the trap door. Deuteronomy was in his assigned place whittling and whistling.

Searching the barn thoroughly, the marshals found the trap

door, and one of them opened it. The stench that emanated from below caused him to slam it back down quickly.

"Your Pa can't be down there," he muttered to the boys.

The two marshals left empty-handed.

Deuteronomy later reported that the boys all got the worst whipping of their lives from a father who was secretly grateful for what they had done.

Reference:

Marsden Durham, "Thus Sayeth the Lord—A Tale of the Underground," *Utah Humanities Review* (October 1947, Vol. 1, No. 4).

PART II: UNFORGETTABLE PERSONALITIES

SHERLOCK HOLMES DEBUTS
AGAINST THE MORMONS

*I*n 1887 Arthur Conan Doyle introduced Sherlock Holmes to the world in the novelette, *A Study in Scarlet*. Holmes went on to become (and still is) the most popular literary detective the world has ever known.

In order to properly launch Holmes into his brilliant career, Doyle needed an auspicious beginning. What better beginning could be devised than by pitting Holmes victoriously against the most insidious evil known in the British world of that day. And what was that evil? In Doyle's mind (and in the minds of many others), it was Mormonism.

The Saints, who now enjoy a growing reputation for being a virtuous and Godly people, were generally considered in the latter half of the 1800s to be the vilest of the vile and the most repugnant of the repugnant. Clearly, any victory Holmes could achieve over such a despised group would elevate him instantly to hero status.

The perceived odium of polygamy was only the beginning. The LDS hierarchy was characterized as requiring absolute and ruthless authority that included murder when necessary to eliminate opposition. Human sacrifice and other abominations were believed to be practiced in their secret temple rites. On more than one occasion, a man would run through the streets of London wearing secret Mormon underwear and brandishing a sword used to decapitate virgins on a sacrificial altar in the Salt Lake Temple. After being ravished, their bodies would then be tossed into the Great Salt Lake. Against such a background environment, Doyle wove his introductory tale.

A Study in Scarlet is divided into two parts. In Part I (seven chapters), Doyle introduces Holmes and has him display his marvelous powers of observation and deduction in solving mysteries. In so doing, he enables the police to apprehend a man named Jefferson Hope who has murdered two other men, Enoch Drebber and Joseph Strangerson.

Doyle uses five chapters of Part 2 to delineate the background leading to the two murders. John Ferrier and his adopted daughter, Lucy, were all who were left of a group of immigrants who had perished in the western American desert of hunger and thirst. Rescued by Mormons, John and Lucy were forced to embrace the Mormon religion and live with their rescuers.

As Lucy developed into young womanhood, a man named Jefferson Hope came onto the scene, and he and Lucy became sweethearts. But when it was decreed that Lucy should become an additional wife of one of two Mormon polygamists who were competing for her hand, the resistance of John, Lucy, and Jefferson met head-on with the absolute authority and control of the Mormon hierarchy .

With Jefferson's help, John and Lucy attempted to escape to Nevada. On the second day of their trek, they made a temporary camp, and Jefferson left John and Lucy to warm themselves by a fire while he went off in search of game. Upon returning to the camp, he found the tragedy that had occurred. "Avenging Angels" had murdered John Ferrier, and there was no trace of

Lucy. Horses' hoof prints, however, showed that the attackers had departed in the direction of Salt Lake City.

Jefferson Hope subsequently learned that Lucy had been forced into a marriage with Enoch Drebber as his eighth wife. Within a month, she died of a broken heart and a broken spirit. Jefferson also learned that Joseph Strangerson, the other contender for Lucy's hand, was the one who had murdered John Ferrier.

Jefferson Hope spent the next twenty years seeking revenge. The trail eventually led him to London where he found and achieved his revenge and where he was ingeniously discovered and apprehended by Sherlock Holmes.

Aside from triumphing over a crime associated with the repugnant Mormons, Holmes endeared himself to the hearts of the readers with his incredible gifts of observation and deduction. Not finding any substantive clues, Inspectors Lestrade and Gregson, of Scotland Yard, welcomed Sherlock Holmes who had been called in to assist. After thoroughly examining the house and grounds where the first murder had been committed, Holmes announced to the astonished assemblage:

> "There has been murder done, and the murderer was a man. He was more than six feet high, was in the prime of life, had small feet for his height, wore coarse, square-toed boots and smoked a Trichinopoly cigar. He came here with his victim in a four-wheeled cab, which was drawn by a horse with three old shoes and one new one on his left fore-leg. In all probability the murderer had a florid face, and the finger nails of his right hand were remarkably long. These are only a few indications, but they may assist you."

Lestrade and Gregson glanced at each other with an incredulous smile.

If this man was murdered, how was it done?" asked the former.

"Poison," said Sherlock Holmes curtly, and strode off.

Holmes not only identified the characteristics of the murderer, he quickly learned the murderer's name (Jefferson Hope) and whereabouts. Holmes then concluded the episode by slapping handcuffs on Hope after decoying Hope to come to him.

No wonder the British readers fell in love with Sherlock Holmes.

The Sherlock Holmes story terminates at this point, but there is a follow-on relationship between Arthur Conan Doyle and the Mormons.

Doyle came to America in 1922 and again in 1923. Although he restricted his first trip to the eastern portions of the United States and Canada, he accepted an invitation from the Salt Lake Knife and Fork Club to visit Salt Lake City on his second trip. The University of Utah Extension Division served as the official host for Doyle's visit. Levi Edgar Young, a Mormon general authority and chairman of the Extension Division, met Doyle at the train station and gave him an introductory tour of the city.

In a speech given in 1953 at Brigham Young University, Young recalled the episode. After being driven around the city for some time, Doyle turned to Young and asked, "When do I get to see some Mormons?"

"Mr. Doyle," Young responded, "most of these people you have been seeing are Mormons. I am a Mormon. And everything you have seen was built by Mormons."

Doyle, who had been expecting to see people with horns, beards, black coats and hats, and grim visages was thoroughly embarrassed.

Doyle stayed in Salt Lake City for two days. On the first night he lectured on Spiritualism to a capacity audience of over 5,000 in the Mormon tabernacle. In his later book, *Our Second American Adventure*, he commented that he had never addressed a more responsive and intelligent audience. Newspaper accounts the next day were glowing in their praise of his address. Doyle was especially impressed with the hospitality he was receiving, especially since many other Christian religions had refused to make their facilities available to him. He further wrote, "It was the more magnanimous because in my early days I had written in *A Study in Scarlet* a rather sensational and over colored picture of the Danite episodes which formed a passing stain in the early history of Utah. This could have easily been brought up to prejudice opinion against me, but as a matter of fact, no allusion was made to it."

Doyle concluded the account of his visit by conceding, "I am ready to think that the ultimate result (of Mormon Doctrine) has been to produce as decent a law-abiding community as is to be found at present in any part of the world. . . . I shall always retain a memory of the tolerance and courtesy which I received in Salt Lake City." As a closing thought, Doyle mentioned the spread of Mormonism into Mexico, California, and other places, and he opined that "the world will be none the worse in consequence."

~

References:

Arthur Conan Doyle, "A Study in Scarlet," *Sherlock Holmes: The Complete Novels and Stories* (New York: Bantam Books, 1986).

Jack Tracy, *Conan Doyle and the Latter-Day Saints* (Bloomington: Gaslight Publications, 1979).

Salt Lake Tribune, May, 1923.

Deseret News, May, 1923.

SAMUEL BRANNON SETS OUT TO
LIBERATE CALIFORNIA

*S*amuel Brannon, an on-again, off-again Mormon, was an entrepreneur. Knowing of the westward migration of the Mormons from Nauvoo, Illinois, Brannon made a proposal to Apostle Orson Pratt, the Mormon authority in the eastern states in 1845. Brannon's idea was to charter a ship and take a company of eastern Saints (as members of The Church of Jesus Christ of Latter-day Saints are called) around Cape Horn and up to California. There they would disembark and travel eastward until they met Brigham Young's westward migration. With Orson Pratt's approval, Brannon and 238 Saints set sail aboard the ship *Brooklyn* on February 4, 1846.

The Saints aboard the *Brooklyn* were of one mind - they were traveling by sea to their Zion where they would finally live in peace. But Samuel Brannon had more grandiose ideas. When they set sail, California was still a province of Mexico, but it appeared inevitable that the United States would extend its boundaries all the way to the Pacific Ocean. So Brannon conceived the idea of "liberating" California from Mexican rule and presenting it to the Unites States. There would be honor and glory in such a feat.

After rounding Cape Horn, Brannon directed the ship to the Hawaiian Islands. Upon docking at Honolulu, he arranged for the purchase of bolts of cloth and related materials, and he put the female passengers to work making military uniforms for the men. Brannon also purchased 150 rifles and other arms. Following about two weeks in Honolulu, the *Brooklyn* embarked for California. En route, Brannon organized the men into military units, gave them close order drill on the ship's decks, and prepared them to overthrow the Mexican garrison upon their arrival at Yerba Buena (now known as San Francisco). But when the *Brooklyn* sailed into San Francisco Bay on July 31, 1846, it was the American flag rather than the Mexican flag that Brannon saw flying above the city's Telegraph Hill.

One can scarcely imagine Brannon's disappointment. "There's that d____d flag again," he muttered. Captain John Montgomery of the American sloop-of-war *Portsmouth* had gotten there 20 days earlier, and he had already displaced the Mexican authorities.

Although Brannon's dream of liberating California was shattered, he had other dreams and he pursued them vigorously. In so doing, he became one of San Francisco's leading citizens. Brannon is credited with bringing law and order to an otherwise lawless settlement. He performed San Francisco's first non-Catholic wedding. He established San Francisco's first newspaper. He built a successful flour mill. He bought property, and he sold property, always at a profit. Although an astute businessman, his philanthropy knew almost no bounds. He was good to the city and to those who lived therein. In pursuing his various enterprises, Sam Brannon became San Francisco's first millionaire.

Perhaps of most significance, Sam Brannon is the person who spread the word about the discovery of gold at Captain John Sutter's lumber mill at Coloma. Brannon did not discover the gold, but he is the one who broadcast its discovery to the world despite Sutter's pleas of secrecy. It may safely be said that it was Brannon who initiated the gold rush of 1849, although had he not been the clarion, someone else would have.

Taking advantage of the great influx of prospectors and entrepreneurs, Brannon bought property and established stores of various kinds in Sacramento and San Francisco. It has been estimated that at one time he owned one-third of Sacramento and one-fourth of San Francisco.

Then, because of an ever-changing environment, Brannon's fortunes reversed, and his speculations went sour. Losing everything, Brannon found himself in poverty and living on borrowed money. He became a recluse and a drunk. His wife gave up on him and went back to her home in Germany. In the end, the Mexican government paid Brannon $49,000 interest on some large sums he had previously loaned to Mexico. To his credit, Brannon used the money to pay his debts. Sadly, Sam Brannon died penniless at the age of seventy.

∽

References:

Irving Stone, *Men to Match My Mountains* (Garden City: Doubleday & Company, Inc. 1956).

Samuel Dickson, *Tales of San Francisco* (Stanford: Stanford University Press, 1957).

Eugene Campbell, "The Apostasy of Samuel Brannon," *Utah Historical Quarterly*, Vol. XXVII, No. 2, April 1959.

JOHN THE BAPTIST: SALT LAKE CITY GRAVE ROBBER

The discovery that Jean Baptiste, a grave digger in the Salt Lake City cemetery, not only dug graves but also reopened them and robbed the bodies, touched off one of the most intense periods of excitement in the annals of that Mormon city. This strange episode is all but forgotten today; however, the passions that were aroused in the winter of 1862 by the discovery of this little man's infamous deeds were such that "the women in their poignant grief would have torn Baptiste into shreds had he not been protected by the iron bars of a prison."

Jean Baptiste, more commonly called "John the Baptist," was reportedly born in Venice, Italy, in 1814. Before coming to Salt Lake City, he had worked as a grave digger in Australia. Coming to Salt Lake City shortly before 1857, Baptiste applied for work at the Salt Lake City cemetery. J. C. Little, City Sexton, gave him a job, and for the next five years the little grave digger quietly plied his trade, hardly being noticed by anyone. But in January 1862, when relatives disinterred the body of Moroni Clawson to remove his remains to another location, Jean Baptiste's secret avocation came to light, and the city at once became the scene of the wildest confusion.

Moroni Clawson had been shot and killed while trying to escape arrest. Since no one came forward at that time to claim Clawson's body, he was buried in the Potter's Field area of the cemetery. Some days later, members of Clawson's family appeared and obtained permission to move the body to a cemetery at Willow Creek (now Draper) in Big Cottonwood Canyon. When the grave was opened, they found themselves staring down at a naked body.

Members of Clawson's family turned their ire on Henry Heath, a Salt Lake City policeman, who had been in charge of the burial. When Henry Clawson accused Heath of improperly burying his brother, Heath became quite upset, for he had not only buried the body in a full set of burial clothes, but he had purchased them with his own money.

"I don't think any pauper ever had cleaner or better burial clothing than he," Heath claimed.

Suspicion soon turned to John Baptiste. Searching Baptiste's home, Heath and fellow policemen found several boxes of clothing and jewelry. They uncovered 60 pairs of children's shoes, a dozen men's shoes, and many items of women's clothing. Baptiste confessed to burying the people in the daytime and then digging them up at night and removing clothing and jewelry. He pled for mercy, but because Heath had recently buried his own daughter in the cemetery, Heath was in no mood to extend mercy. Leading Baptiste to his little girl's grave, Heath demanded, "Did you rob that one?"

"No, no, not that one." Heath later recalled that Baptiste's answer "saved the miserable coward's life."

As news of the grisly discovery spread through Salt Lake City, several citizens remembered passing pawn shop windows and seeing watches, rings, and other items of jewelry that had looked strangely familiar. All the items from Baptiste's house were taken to City Hall and spread out on a table 50 feet long. The mayor declared a city-wide holiday, and citizens stood in line to search the table for items that might have been removed from the bodies of their relatives. The atmosphere was charged with near hysteria, especially as people recognized garments in which their loved ones had been buried. The fact that Baptiste was now incarcerated in the innermost cell of the jail is all that saved him from a lynch mob. Distraught families threatened to open the graves of their deceased to ascertain the condition of the bodies, and if necessary, to reclothe them. The excitement remained high until Brigham Young exerted a calming influence by speaking on the subject in the Tabernacle.

> I will defy any thief there is on the earth or in hell to rob a Saint of one blessing. A thief may dig up dead bodies and sell them for the dissecting knife, or may take their raiment from them, but when the resurrection takes place, the Saints will come forth with all the glory, beauty and excellence of resurrected Saints clothed as they were when they were laid away.
>
> Do as you please with regard to taking up your friends. If I should undertake to do anything of the kind, I should clothe them completely and lay them away again. And if you are afraid of their being robbed again, put them in your gardens where you can watch them.
>
> I would let my friends lay and sleep in peace. The meanness of the act is so far beneath my compre-hension that I have not ventured to think much about it.

Still, what to do with Baptiste. "Hang him," cried some. "Cut his ears off," cried others. Brigham Young suggested that Baptiste simply be exiled and told never to return. Following this suggestion, authorities banished Baptiste to Miller's (now Fremont) Island in the Great Salt Lake. It is known that he remained on the island for several months, then he disappeared and was never seen in Utah again.

~

References:

George U. Hubbard, "Salt Lake City Grave Robber," *True West*, Vol. 13, No. 2, Nov.-Dec. 1965.

Salt Lake Tribune, January 1862.

Deseret News, January 1862.

JOHN D. LEE: PIONEER
EXTRAORDINAIRE

*M*ormon history has such an enormous pioneer heritage that a representative example cannot easily be cited. But because of the diligence of Juanita Brooks in searching out the Mormon experience in southern Utah, there was one pioneer who must not be overlooked. His name was John Doyle Lee.

Among other things, Lee was a diarist. We know more of him than of most individual pioneers because he recorded so much of his experiences and every-day life.

Typical, he was not. As gleaned from his diaries, Lee was 100% converted to the gospel, frequently to the extreme. He was tough, industrious, loyal, and also tender in his attitudes and activity in the Church and towards his family.

John D. Lee was born September 6, 1812, at Kaskaskia, Illinois. He joined the Church in 1838, and he made the trip across the plains in 1848. Lee quickly became a favorite of Brigham Young, and he became one of Brigham Young's adopted children. Typical of his zeal about the gospel, Lee accepted polygamy wholeheartedly. He had 19 wives (not all at the same time), and he fathered 65 children.

After arriving in the Salt Lake Valley, Lee built a home for himself and his family, and then almost immediately he left it to respond to a call to go south and help in colonizing southern Utah. The majority of his years were spent in the Harmony and Washington communities.

Unfortunately, Lee is now remembered primarily for his role in the Mountain Meadows Massacre, a tragedy for which he was the only person convicted and executed. But in his earlier years on the frontier, he was in a class by himself. Let's sample Lee's earlier years.

John D. Lee loved his family, and he was especially kind and tender to his wives. When his first wife, Aggatha, was ill and dying, Lee described the occasion poignantly. (Note: An attempt has here been made to preserve the spelling and punctuation in Lee's diary notations.)

 This Morning Agga More restless. Severe Pains in her shoulders; her life is now despaird off. About 10 morning M. H. Darrow startd to cannaraville for Almy, Ann and children & Mary Leah my wife & children & son. Returned about 6 Eving with the companions. When they arrived we thought Agga was Dying, but on hearing that her children had come, she revived & was set up a few moments & talked to them in a kind & touching Manner which would Melt the hardest Heart. At this Moment Jos. returned with a bucket of Snow (at the request of his Mother) which he got in the Mountain 4 ms. off. As he came in, she took a Mouthful of the snow, relished it & Said, Here comes Jos. Jos, you are good Boy. This Snow tasts so good & cooling to me. Then took the children by the hand, one by one. My children are all here save S. Jane, she said, & I want to talk to you, my Dear children. I can not be much longer with you, I am going to rest, & soon you will be without a Mother. But remember that you have a good Father.

Aggatha went on to exhort her children to live the gospel and obey their father. Two days later she "yeilded up the Ghost."

Lee expressed himself tenderly with the following poem which he composed and placed on Aggatha's tombstone:

> She has gone to the Rest
> The companion of my youth
> Her spirit now is blest
> With them that love the truth
> Before her spirit left its clay
> She called her children near
> And wisely unto them did say
> Obey your Father Dear
> He'll never council you amiss
> Through all your future Life
> Then gave unto each one a Kiss
> O, She was a Mother & a Wife.

Yes, Lee was kind and loving to his wives, but when certain occasions arose, he could also be quite dictatorial. On one occasion in Nauvoo, when Lee and Aggatha were preparing for the trek to the west some of Aggatha's relatives tried to persuade her not to go. Lee laid down the law. Lee told her that if she intended to look to him for protection and salvation, that "she must adhere to his counsel for he was her Husband, Brother, Father, President, & Savior or else he was nothing."

As one of the leaders in colonizing southern Utah, Lee spent a large portion of his life in the area around Harmony, Utah. He worked hard. He was prosperous, and he was generous. He built a large home which became a frequent gathering place for social events. In his diary Lee records details of a Fourth of July (1858) celebration in which "some 400 persons took breakfast in my family hall at my expense."

Lee also served an afternoon meal and then another breakfast the next morning. A day earlier he butchered 2,000 pounds of meat for the occasion. Lee wrote that altogether he and his family served a total of over 900 meals. Only in an extremely well organized household could this happen.

Medical practitioners and medicinal remedies were scarce during those frontier times, and the pioneers had to use innovative and unusual practices at times. At one time, Lee was in bed for two weeks with a debilitating infection that would not go away. "Finally," he wrote in his diary,

> Spirits of Turpentine, coal oil, Dr. Lee's linement, Salt Peter, wild sage & vinegar, Roast Onions & carrots, white Beans, Mountain soap, Champhor & Salt, & last of all . . . a Poltice of charcoal & carrots grated. This together with the Prayer of Faith seemed to check the inflamation & gave me ease.

On another occasion his sheep were sick and dying.

> I dockerd them with everything that I could think, but in vain. 12 head died. About dark I remembered that the Lord Said in a rev. that Tobacco was good for sick cattle. So I tried it, steeped it in hot water & drenched some 10 sheep that had lain all day almost lifeless & to my astonishment they all recovered; which was to me a valuable Piece of information.

John D. Lee was a pioneer. He was a colonizer. And above all, he was a family man. Even though he operated on a larger scale than most of his contemporaries, he symbolized the pioneer spirit of the early LDS colonizers.

❦

Reference:

Juanita Brooks, *A Mormon Chronicle: The Diaries of John D. Lee* (San Marino: The Huntington Library, 1955), Vols. 1 &2.

CHIEF WALKER DOESN'T GET
HIS WAY

*D*uring the early days of Manti, Utah, the Paiute Indians living in that area acknowledged allegiance to two chiefs, the old and venerable Chief Sowiatt and the younger and more belligerent Chief Walker.

On one occasion, most of Manti's male population was away, some working at Hamilton's saw mill on Pleasant Creek, and others away on business or for other reasons. Only 10 or 15 men remained in Manti that day. Chief Walker, in one of his bad moods, picked that time to impose his belligerence on the white people of Manti.

Wearing his war paint, Walker demanded that two of the men remaining in town, Shumway and Chase, be delivered to him immediately. The reasons for the selection of these two men, whom Walker would execute, are unknown. Of course the people in Manti refused to comply with such a demand, and they braced themselves for whatever might come.

Walker probably would have come in force for the two men had not Chief Sowiatt taken issue with such a plan. In a council meeting, Walker addressed his braves, appealing to their basest passions. It seemed that a universal slaughter was imminent. Sowiatt then rose and chided the tribe for wanting to go against "squaws and papooses," and with eloquence he called upon them to recognize the cowardice and shame of what they were contemplating.

Then with a stick, Sowiatt drew a line in the soil, and he challenged the braves, "Those who will live in friendship with the Mormons, let them follow me." As he stepped across the line, the majority of braves rose and followed him. Walker silently stole away and sulked until his "mood" passed.

Because of Chief Sowiatt's actions, Manti was saved, and peaceful relations ensued.

~

Reference:

Mrs. A. B. Sidwell, *Reminiscences of Early Days in Manti* (1889).

WOVOKA AND THE GHOST DANCE: THE INDIANS' LAST GREAT HOPE

In the winter of 1887-1888, a relatively unknown, nondescript Paiute Indian named Wovoka fell into a trance, went to heaven, was instructed by God, and returned to promote a new Messianic religion among the Indians of the western United States. Wovoka, whose Anglo name was Jack Wilson, had been a visionary man in the past, and he already had a reputation as a seer and a prophet among the Indians of western Nevada. His new messiahship, however, began in earnest following the experience of his trance.

For three days he lay lifeless. Friends and family urged his wife, Mary, to bury him, but she steadfastly said, "No! He will come awake, but only when God tells him so."

Then on the third day he awoke and announced to all that he had been in God's presence and that he was sent back to teach a new way of life to the Indians.

Two days later, after regaining strength, Wovoka called the local Indians together to tell them about his three-day sojourn in heaven. For over an hour, Wovoka spoke about his experience in heaven and the things he had been commanded to teach to the people. He taught that the time was near for the Indians to be united and restored to their former state of glory. They would enter into a state of eternal bliss, free from the oppressions of the white men. It was a message of restoration. It was a message of hope for all Indians.

"I saw Indians of every tribe, of every nation, walking arm-in-arm like brothers. One time they were enemies. Now they are as one. I saw the flowering of human beauty; the end of all pain and disease. And I saw man win his last bad struggle with death. In that great land the Indian is not the slave, nor beaten dog, of the white man. There he stands tall and handsome—the equal of all."

In addition, Wovoka reported that in the world he saw, there would be no death. "The dead are all alive again. When your loved ones die, there must be no more crying. And Jesus Christ will be your heavenly Messiah."

Wovoka was instructed to return to earth and teach the people that to gain the paradise he had seen, they would have to make improvements to their way of life.

"You must teach them that they must not hurt anyone, or do harm to any living thing. They must not drink whiskey. They must not fight. Always they must do right. They must not refuse to work for the whites."

To add emphasis to this message, Wovoka was instructed to introduce a dance (which became known as the Ghost Dance) among the Indian tribes, "It is the dance of the spirits. It is the dance of goodness. It is a dance from heaven. It has a purpose. It will make your people free. It will make your people glad."

Although Wovoka's message visualized eventual Indian supremacy and the overthrow of their subjugation by the white man, it was also a message of peace and love and honorable living along with a glorious eternity.

An earthly Messiah was needed to maintain communication with God and to give direction to the people. Although Wovoka's teachings had a close similarity to the teachings being delivered by the Mormon missionaries in Nevada, he rejected Joseph Smith as the Paiute's prophet. How could the Indians hope to gain ascendency over the whites by adopting a white man's religion? "If Paiutes need a prophet, I am that prophet," he is quoted as saying. "I am a Paiute. This Joseph Smith, he is white man. I say that Paiutes should have a Paiute prophet. I, Wovoka —son of Tavibo—am that man."

Wovoka's claims of earthly messiahship were generally accepted in his local environment, but in outlying areas throughout the west, he remained a relatively unknown quantity. Therefore, he attracted little attention except in western Nevada where he was well known. For two years he met with mediocre success. Then his big opportunity came.

In 1889 Wovoka contracted a fever and fell into a second trance. But this time the circumstances were decidedly in his favor. His trance coincided with a solar eclipse, and he awoke from this trance just as the sun was reemerging. As a result he quickly became known throughout the western tribes as the Indian prophet who controlled the sky and brought the sun back to life. His missionaries went out to spread his gospel, and his fame was now assured. The western tribes now recognized one of their own who could truly lead them in restoring their lost dignity and glory.

From this second trance, Wovoka's message was a continuation from what it had been. The Earth would be destroyed by flood, and then returned to its paradisiacal glory. "Soon the earth shall die. But Indians need not be afraid. It is the white men, not Indians, who should be afraid, for they will be wiped from the face of the earth by a mighty flood of mud and water. Then when the flood has passed, the earth will come alive again. The land will be new and green with young grass. Elk and deer and antelope and even the vanished buffalo will return in vast numbers as they were before the white men came. And all

Indians will be young again and free of the white man's sick-
nesses. It will be a paradise on earth."

Along with the vision, God placed major emphasis on
renewing the Ghost Dance. Participation in the dance was
required to strengthen the Indians' commitment in, and hope for,
their promised ascendency.

The Ghost Dance was a circular dance of both males and
females. Some tribes danced around a pole or a tree, while others
used nothing in the center of the circle. Slowly the circle rotated
in a clockwise direction as the dancers, with holy symbols painted
on their faces, entwined their hands and moved from right to left.
The steps were simple and stately. As the left foot advanced to the
left, the right foot moved to where the left had been, while
keeping time to songs.

Wovoka's message and his messiahship now spread like wild-
fire. Numerous tribes sent emissaries to meet with Wovoka and to
learn from him. The Indians of the west now had a new-found
hope. Visitors came from all over. The Bannocks and the
Shoshones in Idaho played major roles in spreading the message.
From as far away as Indian Territory (now Oklahoma), the
Arapahos sent a delegation. The Sioux in the Dakotas became
fervent adherents. Included among other tribes adopting the
Ghost Dance were the Cheyenne, Mandan, Ute, Caddo,
Comanche, Kiowa, Pawnee, Delaware, Iowa, Kansas, Kickapoo,
Wichita, and many others. Throughout almost the entire West,
Indian tribes accepted the new Messiah and sought to hasten the
fulfillment of his promises by dancing the Ghost Dance.

As the dance spread, various tribes made their own additions
to the original ritual as taught by Wovoka. The primary concept,
however, remained a constant. In all tribes, the fundamental
purpose of the dance was to hasten the day of millennial peace
and happiness. According to Mooney, who became an authority
on the Ghost Dance, "The great and underlying principle of the
Ghost Dance doctrine is that the time will come when the whole

Indian race, living and dead, will be reunited upon a regenerated earth, to live a life of aboriginal happiness, forever free of death, disease, and misery.'

Frequently the dance became an ordeal of endurance. In many tribes it was a five-day dance as taught by Wovoka. Indians that dropped out from exhaustion were replaced by others. In many cases, songs and hypnotic trances linked the physical dancing to the more spiritual objectives of the dance.

With some, the dance was performed on ground hallowed by a pre-dance dedication ceremony. Some tribes preceded the dance with song and with a purification ritual referred to by whites as a "sweat bath." In many tribes, the dance required fasting by the participants.

Another feature of the Ghost Dance rituals was a ceremonial garment, or shirt, which constituted a protective shield for the wearer. The men of many tribes, and especially the Sioux, wore these decorated shirts as a sacred protection against harm or death from the white men. In song they referred to the protective properties of the shirts.

Verily I have given you my strength,
Verily I have given you my strength,
Says the father.
Says the father.
The shirt will cause you to live,
The shirt will cause you to live,
Says the father.
Says the father.

As the Ghost Dance spread throughout the western and central tribes, the Indians' intentions, as taught by Wovoka, were noble and peaceful. But government officials, on the other hand, looked upon the rapid spread of this movement with considerable alarm. They became especially wary as they watched the infusion of the dance into the rebellious Sioux nation.

Within the Sioux nation, Sitting Bull and Red Cloud had finally accepted Wovoka's messiahship, and they looked upon the movement as a beginning of the liberation they so desperately wanted. Believing that by peaceful means they would finally be freed of the white man's oppression and double-dealing, they made the Ghost Dance a popular feature on the Pine Ridge and Rosebud reservations. But the Indian agent, already apprehensive of the Sioux's warlike tendencies, feared that another uprising might be forming, and he ordered the dance stopped. For a while the Sioux complied with the cease and desist order, but when they noted further changes and indecisiveness among the government agents, they resumed the dance. In October 1890, Kicking Bear, the chief high priest of the Ghost Dance among the Sioux, went by invitation to Standing Rock to inaugurate the dance on Sitting Bull's own reservation. Refusing government orders to again discontinue he dance, Sitting Bull added to the government's long-standing mistrust of him. Rather than risk another uprising, the government officials decided that Sitting Bull would have to be arrested and removed from his position of influence among his people. And so it was that as preparations for the Ghost Dance were being made on the Standing Rock reservation, government officials and Indian police attempted on December 15, 1890, to arrest Sitting Bull. In the ensuing fracas, Sitting Bull was shot and killed.

Two weeks later the Battle of Wounded Knee occurred. Riding into battle wearing their ceremonial protective garments which were supposed to protect them from harm and death, the Indian warriors were massacred. Short Bull, who had been one of the Sioux delegates to Wovoka, later asked, "Who would have thought that dancing could make such trouble? For the message that I brought was peace. And the message was given by the Father to all the tribes."

With these two tragedies among the Sioux, the Ghost Dance began to fade in popularity, and the Indians' last hope of redemption from the oppression of the white men died.

References:

James Mooney, *The Ghost Dance* (North Dighton, MA: JG Press, 1996).

David Humphreys Miller, *Ghost Dance* (Lincoln, NE: University of Nebraska Press, 1959).

Paul Bailey, *Ghost Dance Messiah* (Tucson, Westernlore Press, 1986).

Raymond J. DeMallie and Douglas R. Parks, Eds, *Sioux Indian Religion* (Norman: University of Oklahoma Press, 1987).

BUTCH CASSIDY: ROBIN HOOD OF THE WEST

utch Cassidy was different. Unlike most of the other western outlaws, it is believed that he never killed anyone. It is also believed that he outdid all the others with regard to cattle rustling and bank and train robberies. But Cassidy also had a streak of humanity that endeared him to many who were down on their luck or oppressed by others. Butch has often been referred to as the "Robin Hood of the West" as a result of various escapades of taking from the rich and giving to the poor.

Cassidy, born to a Latter-day Saint family, was actually named Robert LeRoy Parker. His parents and grandparents had come across the plains as pioneers. He was raised in a gospel environment. But the pioneer life, with its drudgery and insecurity, was not for him. He was going to be a noted leader of something, of anything. And so, despite the pleas of his mother, he left home at the age of eighteen to conquer the world.

Butch did become a leader. He did become famous. To some, he became the best (or worst depending on one's perspective) of the bad men of the west. To others, he was a true Robin Hood, taking from the rich and giving to the poor. And sometimes he was able to combine these two roles in a single escapade. A case in point –

A certain farmer (whose name has been forgotten) for whom Butch had developed a feeling of fondness had fallen on hard times. His crops had not been successful, he was behind on his mortgage to the bank, and the bank had announced a foreclosure on his property. That meant that the farmer and his family would lose everything they had worked for and built over the years. They would be destitute, having lost all. When Butch heard of the upcoming foreclosure, he quickly decided he was not going to let that happen.

So what did Butch do? He went to the bank, and with his own money he paid off the mortgage and obtained the deed and other associated legal documents. He then rode out to the farm and presented the deed to an astonished and grateful farmer and his wife. The farm was now theirs, free and clear. They were the sole owners. The bank had no more claim on their property. The second half of a Robin Hood sequence had been performed.

What do you think Cassidy did next? The next day he went back to the same bank and robbed it. Taking out the exact amount of money he put in the day before, he went on his way. The Robin Hood sequence was now complete.

∼

Reference:

Kathryn Jenkins Gordon, *Butch Cassidy and Other Mormon Outlaws of the Old West* (American Fork, Utah: Covenant Communications, Inc., 2013.

PANCHO VILLA BEFRIENDS THE MORMONS

*I*n the late 1800s when the Federal government was trying to stamp out the Saints' practice of plural marriage, many polygamous families moved to Mexico to escape persecutions and imprisonment by U.S. marshals. By 1885 several permanent colonies were established in the northern Mexican states of Chihuahua and Sonora, the largest and most prominent colonies being Colonia Juarez and Colonia Dublan.

From the inception of these colonies, the Saints in Mexico attempted to be exemplars of good citizenship. Their homes and towns were clean, neat, and attractively landscaped. For the most part, they established prosperous and self-sustaining communities with flocks and herds, farms and orchards. In 1896 they displayed their wares in a Mexican national fair and won the admiration of Mexican President Porfirio Diaz.

The Saints also made special efforts of neutrality during the troubled times of the Mexican revolution which began in 1910 and continued for approximately ten years. By 1912, armed conflicts were occurring throughout northern Mexico, and despite their proximity to these conflicts, the LDS colonists avoided taking sides.

It is believed that Pancho Villa, one of the leading revolutionaries, had frequent contact with the Saints during his escapades in Chihuahua. For the most part he left them alone, and they left him alone. But there was one situation, occurring in 1916, when the colonists of Colonia Dublan feared an attack from Villa who had declared his wrath on all Americans.

In attempting to win control of the Mexican state of Sonora, Villa attacked Federalist forces at Auga Prieta, just south of the New Mexico border. Villa was soundly defeated, however, by a superior army that was much larger and stronger than he had anticipated. As a result Pancho Villa was furious!! His anger was directed toward the United States whose leaders he blamed for the defeat he and his forces had just suffered.

The United States had allowed Mexican Federalist soldiers to enter Texas at Eagle Pass and then travel by train over United States soil through El Paso and into New Mexico to reinforce the Sonoran defenders below the border. Villa's force could not compete with these unexpected reinforcements.

After being mauled and defeated at Auga Prieta in Sonora, Villa gave vent to his rage by raiding Columbus, New Mexico, as a token of retaliation against the United States.

"We're going to kill gringos," Villa told his decimated troops on the eve of the attack.

Galloping into Columbus early in the morning of March 9, 1916, Villa's forces sacked and burned the hotel, the grocery stores, and several other buildings. They also killed at least seventeen Americans.

After raiding Columbus, Villa's planned route back to his headquarters led directly through the Saints' colony of Colonia Dublan. Having been neutral throughout the revolutionary period, the residents hoped that Villa would continue to leave them alone. But they nevertheless were Americans, and Villa had vowed retribution on any Americans. As his army neared the area of Colonia Dublan, the Saints there sensed possible danger, and they held a strategy meeting to discuss alternative actions. Many suggestions came forth.

"Let's defend ourselves with our deer rifles and shotguns."

"Let's take our wives and families into the mountains."

"Let's set up an ambush for them."

"Let's dynamite them."

After listening to these proposals, Bishop Anson Call stood up and said, "I think we ought to go home, have prayers, turn out the lights, go to bed, and leave it in the hands of the Lord." Further discussion followed, until one by one, the assemblage disbursed and did as the Bishop had recommended.

That night (at 3:00 am), Villa and his forces arrived at the edge of the valley. Holding up his hand, Villa is reported to have announced, "There's an ambush. I can see the lights of fires all throughout the valley."

The other rebel leaders, who were riding close to Villa, declared that they could not see any such thing.

Villa, however, continued to insist that he saw lights, and as a result he directed his army to detour around the valley. They went on their way, leaving the colonists alone. Apparently the prayers and fasting of the Saints was not in vain.

A more direct contact between Pancho Villa and the Saints occurred three years later. With several pairs of proselyting missionaries located in nearby towns and villages, it was the practice of the Church leaders to make periodic visits to the missionaries to tend to their spiritual and temporal needs. In March 1919, a party of three LDS leaders set out on such a journey. They were Joseph C. Bentley, President of the Juarez Stake, James Elbert Whetton, Supervisor of mission activity in that area, and Albert Tiatjua. Although they had passports guaranteeing safe passage through rebel-held territory, they were stopped by rebels while traveling from Buenaventura southward to Namiquipa. The rebels held their captives for a few days and then took them to Pancho Villa's base camp a few miles away. Knowing of Villa's current attitude toward Americans, and knowing that their captives were Americans, the rebels anxiously wondered what Villa would do with them. Being kindly disposed toward the Saints in general, Villa surprised his followers. Instead of ordering the execution of these prisoners, he invited them to breakfast. Villa also invited his friend and co-leader, General Felipe Angeles, to join them.

The breakfast conversation consisted primarily of questions by General Angeles about the Church and its teachings, and responses and explanations by Elder Whetton who was fully fluent with the Spanish language. Villa was frequently in and out of the room, but when there, he listened intently. At a later date, on July 18, 1932, Elder Whetton dictated an account of these experiences to Joseph Franklin Moffett whose typescript account is on file in the archives of The Church of Jesus Christ of Latter-day Saints. Extracted from Whetton's account to Moffett are the following statements attributed to Pancho Villa.

"I want you to give my regards and best wishes to all the Mormon people and tell them that they can expect to have as much help and protection from me and my men as it is possible for me to give them in times of trouble. They have been my friends and I want them to feel that I am their friend."

This is quite a statement considering Villa's antagonistic feelings toward Americans in general. Villa also added, "When we get this affair settled I would like to see the influence of Mormon communities in every part of this republic."

Additional extracts of the breakfast conversation have been printed in the Church Section of the *Deseret News* for November 11, 1967.

Pancho Villa: "I always admired the Mormon people. They don't interfere. They are good people and mind their own business."

General Angeles to Villa: "General, for my part I wish the whole Republic would turn Mormon. When this revolution is settled, I am going to join this church if there is an opportunity for me to do it."

Pancho Villa to President Bentley: "Why haven't any of your people explained these things to me before? This is the first time I have known anything about your teachings. If I had known these things when I was younger, my life would have been different. Is there a chance for a man like me to join the Mormon Church?"

After breakfast Villa gave the "prisoners" new passports and bid them farewell. To President Bentley, Villa said, "I want you to give my regards and best wishes to all of the Mormon people and tell them that they can expect to have as much help and protection from me and my men as it is possible for me to give them in these times of trouble. They have been my friends and I want them to feel that I am their friend."

Elder Whetton thanked Villa for his kindnesses and said, in parting, "If there is ever any time when I can do something for you, I will do it." Thus ended the episode,--almost.

The rest of the story has been gleaned primarily from the aforementioned Church Section of the *Deseret News*. Because Villa and General Angeles, now both dead, had been such good friends to the Saints, President Bentley wrote to Church President Heber J. Grant making a plea for temple work to be done for them. President Grant approved the requests, but for some reason, the ordinances were not performed. A few years passed, and President Bentley died. Then one night, Pancho Villa (whose real name was Jose Dorotea Arango) appeared to Elder Whetton.

"Do you know me?" Villa asked.

"Si"

"You told me that if there was ever any time you could do something for me, you would do it. You are the only one who can help me. I want you to do my temple work."

Feeling the need of family support, Elder Whetton visited

Pancho Villa's widow who was in full support of the proposed temple ordinances. During the visit she stated that her husband's life "had been changed by the Mormon Elders."

Permission was again received from Salt Lake City, and on February 25, 1966, Jose Dorotea Arango was baptized by proxy in the Mesa Arizona Temple. A few days later Elder Whetton was endowed for Villa. Similar temple work was also done for Felipe Angeles.

References:

Robert E. Wells, "In God We Trust," an address given at Brigham Young University on June 29, 1982.

"Mexico," *Collier's Encyclopedia*, 1964.

Laura King and Amparo Garcia, "Mormons Find Sanctuary in Mexico in 1880s," Internet article.

Joseph Franklin Moffett, "Captured by General Villa," dictated by James Elbert Whetton, typescript in the Church Archives and Library in Salt Lake City, Utah.

David K. Martineau, *Hey Gringo! What Are You Doing Here* (Bradenton, Florida: BookLocker.com, 2015).

Joseph Franklin Moffett, *General Pershing, Pancho Villa and the Mormons in Mexico*, typescript in the Church Archives and Library in Salt Lake City, Utah.

Charles H. Harris, *Pancho Villa and the Columbus Raid: The Missing Documents*, pamphlet in the Church Archives and Library in Salt Lake City, Utah.

"Church Section," *Deseret News*, November 11, 1967.

INA COOLBRITH HELPS LAUNCH
SEVERAL WRITING CAREERS

*I*f you have not heard of Ina Coolbrith, you have missed becoming acquainted with a woman of very special qualities. Ina's is a story of both accomplishment and mystery. Known through most of her life as Ina Coolbrith, her real name was Josephina Donna Smith. She was the daughter of Don Carlos and Agnes Smith, and therefore a niece of the Prophet Joseph Smith. Her's is a fascinating story, both with regard to her name change and with regard to her many accomplishments in the world of early California literature.

Born on March 10, 1841, in Nauvoo, Illinois, Josephine was the third child of Don Carlos and Agnes Smith. Two sisters, Agnes and Sophronia, had preceded her. Life in Nauvoo at that time had been good, and Don Carlos and Agnes were delighted with this new addition to their family. Then tragedy began to strike. Don Carlos died, presumably of pneumonia, five months after Josephine's birth. Then two years later in 1843, scarlet fever claimed Sophronia, leaving Agnes doubly desolate. The tragedies continued. Joseph and Hyrum were martyred in 1844. Samuel Harrison, another brother of Don Carlos, died also in 1844 from exposures he had suffered in the persecutions. When the Saints began leaving Nauvoo in 1845, the widowed Agnes had a decision to make.

Agnes had endured the persecutions in Ohio and in Missouri. When a mob destroyed her home in the Far West area, Agnes waded the icy Grand River with a daughter under each arm and trekked three miles in a snow storm seeking safety and shelter. Finally finding peace in Nauvoo, Illinois, the Saints had a period of peace and comfort and happiness. But now the persecutions were happening all over again.

The thought of facing another migration, and this time without the emotional and physical support of Don Carlos, was too much. Agnes was bereft and tired. Wanting peace and tranquility, she chose to stay behind, as Emma and Lucy had also done.

Agonizing over her decision to stay, Agnes penned a letter to Apostle (and cousin) George A. Smith in which she lamented:

 I have no other one to ask but you. My mind is much troubled about coming to the Camp. I want to come and I do not want to come. I feel alone - all alone. If there was a Carlos or Joseph or Hyrum then how quickly would I be there.

I love the Church of Christ. I love to be with my brethren, but alas, there is an aching void that I seem never able to fill.

I have sold the old printing office for seventy dollars. I have had my dead removed into Emma's garden.

May the Lord bless you all is my prayer.

Agnes M. Smith

As the Saints were moving out of Nauvoo, other people were

moving in. One of those newcomers was a printer from St. Louis named William Picket. He came to Nauvoo initially to observe the hostilities, and he became thoroughly disgusted with the repugnant behavior of the non-Mormon element. Being a fearless man with a strong sense of compassion for the oppressed, Pickett, a non-Mormon himself, became embroiled in the difficulties still existing for Mormons in and about the city of Nauvoo. Since William Pickett was a printer and Agnes Smith was the widow of a printer with a printing shop on her hands, it seems natural that the two should meet and form a relationship. Not only did they meet, they become friends, and then they married in the summer of 1846.

Following their marriage, the Picketts moved to St. Louis where, in December 1847, Agnes and William were blessed with twin boys who they named William Pickett, Jr. and Don Carlos Pickett. The name of the latter twin gives an indication of the strong attachment Agnes still held for her first husband. It also speaks well for William Pickett, who was willing to honor Agnes' first husband in such a permanent manner. Agnes and William were now the parents of four living children: Agnes Charlotte and Josephine from Agnes' marriage to Don Carlos Smith, and now the new twins.

The Pickett's sojourn in St. Louis was cut short by the lure of gold in California. William did not necessarily want to be a miner, but perhaps he could work there for a while as a printer and then migrate to his desired profession practicing law. Therefore, in 1852, the Pickett family joined a California-bound wagon train. All went well on the first part of the journey, but ironically, the wagon train camped for the winter on the outskirts of Salt Lake City. So Agnes found herself again in the midst of friends and relatives who urged her to stay. But when the wagon train moved on, Agnes and her children went with them,

The Picketts settled first in southern California, in Los Angeles and in San Bernardino. In his desire to become a lawyer,

William Pickett felt that his chances of success would be greatly hindered if the Mormon background of his family were known. So at his insistence, Agnes agreed to keep that part of her heritage a secret, and she bound her children to the same pledge of secrecy. The pledge included dropping the surname of Smith. The name change came easily for Josephine who, as a teenager, was already writing and publishing poems in the *Los Angeles Star* and signing them "Ina." Taking her mother's maiden name as her own, Josephine Donna Smith became Ina Donna Coolbrith.

Through her poetry in the *Star*, Ina became a favorite among the populace. Her popularity was in evidence when Pío Pico, the former Mexican governor of California chose her to be his partner in leading the grand march at a formal ball. "He danced divinely," she later recalled.

But there were also heartaches and disappointments for Ina. A failed marriage and the death of an infant child took a toll that remained with Ina throughout her celebrated life. A touch of melancholy showed itself in many of her later poems.

Ina's experience in Los Angeles ended when William Pickett decided to move the family to San Francisco in 1862. The move proved to be a new and very successful beginning for Ina and her literary pursuits. She met Bret Harte and the two of them plus Charles Warren Stoddard became editors of the literary journal, *The Overland Monthly*. Known as "The Overland Trinity," they won the praise of the more erudite eastern critics. The three of them loved and respected one another, and it was here that Ina began to exert her influence on those about her.

A case in point centers around a story Bret Harte wrote. While still unpublished, Harte complained to Ina about a lady proof-reader who refused to work on a story he had written for the *Overland Monthly*. Dejected by the proof-reader's vehement complaint about the story's low moral quality, Harte decided to withdraw it. Ina read the story and liked it.

"It's a good story," she proclaimed. "Don't you dare withdraw it. We're going to print it."

As a result, "The Luck of Roaring Camp" saw the light of day, and Brett Harte's writing career was launched.

Poetry came naturally to Ina. During some light-hearted repartee following their initial success with "The Luck," Ina teased Harte, (whose real given name was Francis), by singing out the following spontaneous limerick:

> *There was a young writer names Francis,*
> *Who concocted such lurid romances,*
> *That his publishers said,*
> *"You'll strike this firm dead,*
> *If you don't put a curb to your fancies."*

Harte instantly retorted:

> *There is a poetic divinity—*
> *Number One of the "Overland Trinity"—*
> *Who uses the muses*
> *Pretty much as she chooses--*
> *This dark eyed, young Sapphic divinity.*

Such was the enjoyment they had with one another.

Ina's years on the *Overland* staff were among her happiest. Her world was the literary world, and she was mingling with those people who constituted California's "Golden Age" of literature. And through her own poetry she was an equal and an admired contributor. Not only did they fully accept her, they made her their companion, hostess, tutor, and critic. The parlor of Ina's home on Taylor Street became the gathering place for the local literary element. And visitors such as Mark Twain, Robert Louis Stevenson, Rudyard Kipling, and Joaquin Miller made it a point to be there when in town.

It was in Ina's parlor that Joaquin Miller began his poetic

assent. On his first visit, he was a rather nondescript looking young poet whose real name was Cincinatus Hiner Miller and whose poems had been rejected by a publisher. Discouraged, Miller asked Ina for counsel and advice.

"How in the world," she declared, "do you ever expect to climb Parnassus with such a name as you have?"

Ina thought of the famous bandit Joaquin Murrieta, whose name she felt had a musical ring. She then rechristened the would-be poet Joaquin Miller, and he successfully resubmitted his poems. Ina had successfully helped launch another literary career.

They say that it is a long road that never turns. While Ina was basking in her glory, her road began to turn. William Pickett disappeared into the gold fields and was never heard from again. Ina's mother, Agnes, was ailing. Her sister, Agnes Charlotte was married and living in Los Angeles. Her two brothers were no help. Ina assumed the responsibilities of keeping the family going. She had to go to work and become the bread-winner. In 1874 at the age of thirty-three, Ina became the librarian of the Oakland Public Library. This meant that her production of poetry would be severely diminished, but her influence on others would continue. But now she would be helping aspiring youth.

Ina took a personal interest in a particular fourteen year old waif who regularly visited the library and devoured everything he could read. She was always happy to see that boy, and she guided his choice of readings. Later in his life, this waif wrote the following to Ina:

 The old Oakland library days! Do you know you were the first one who ever complimented me on my choice of reading matter.... Proud! If you only knew how proud your words made me! You were a goddess to me.

When I hear your name mentioned, or think of

you, up at once flashes that memory picture, and with it its connotation, and its connotation is "Noble!" Often and often the mere word "noble" recalls you to my mind.

The name of the boy? Jack London.

Ina gave similar encouragement to an appreciative young girl named Isadora Duncan. Later, as a world famous dancer, Isadora wrote in her autobiography:

> I ran or danced or skipped there (to the library) and back. The librarian was a very wonderful and beautiful woman, a poetess of California, Ina Coolbrith. She encouraged my reading, and I thought she always looked pleased when I asked for fine books.

Even though severely restricted in her poetic output, Ina managed to publish the first of three books of poetry. When her book, *A Perfect Day, and Other Poems*, appeared in 1881, it was well received in the East and in England.

The poems "have the singing quality, and besides being musical are very daintily expressed. The utterances of a true poet who, like the robin, sings because she must," wrote the *Boston Courier*.[10] The *Philadelphia Press* wrote: "This is something more than a mere book of verse; there is about it the atmosphere of a higher thought and a truer aspiration than is usual in the average volume of rhymes." *Vanity Fair* commented that "there is refined motion, the constant yearning sentiment, the poetic wish and realization, and the form of noble music." Even Longfellow is reported to have remarked: "I know that California has at least one poet. Her publisher sent me a book of Ina Coolbrith's poems, and I have been reading them with delight."

Ina's fame spread to England. In a four page article written by Albert Kinross, editor of the *London Outlook*, Kinross proclaimed "Here is a poet." Kinross went on to write, "She is as inspired a writer of verse as any now alive." As a result of the *Outlook*'s introduction, English journals began printing Ina's poetry, and some of her poems, having been set to music, were sung on London stages. She became acquainted with Rudyard Kipling. Lord Alfred Tennyson is said to have corresponded with her. George Meredith once remarked to a visitor from America, "Why doesn't Ina Coolbrith come to London to live? When you go home you tell her she is one of the few lyric poets who have impressed me."

One of the highlights of Ina's life was her visit in 1884 to John Greenleaf Whittier, the Quaker poet, at his home in Danvers, Massachusetts. The two had corresponded over the years, and Whittier had been impressed with Ina's poetry, so much so that he memorized her lengthy poem, "California" in its entirety. It was an extremely warm and cordial visit in which Whittier invited Ina to remain in the East and live in his house which he shared with three female cousins. Ina, however, felt the necessity of returning to her California home, but as she parted at the end of her visit, Whittier said, "I want thee to remember that so long as he lives Whittier's home is thine whenever and for as long as thee should require or desire it."

Ina published her second book of poems in 1895. The book, *Songs from the Golden Gate*, brought further praise and compensated in large measure for the decrease in poetic output caused by the necessity of work and by old age. But the esteem with which she was blessed continued unabated. The pinnacle of her poetic career occurred in 1919 when the State of California bestowed on her its highest honor. The California Legislature passed a bill declaring Ina "Loved Laurel-Crowned Poet of California."

The mystery of Ina's Mormon heritage, which had lain fallow for so many years began to emerge in her later years. It is true that one cousin, Joseph F. Smith, president of The Church of Jesus Christ of Latter-day Saints knew of Ina, and he even visited her on at least two occasions. But it was up to another cousin, Jesse Winter Smith, grandson of Samuel H. Smith, to become actively involved. As a student at Stanford University in Palo Alto, Uncle J (as he later became known) deduced Ina's true identity, and he determined to visit her. The visit was made early in 1906, just before the San Francisco earthquake. The following is Smith's verbal account of the visit.

> Yes, I visited Ina Coolbrith in her home one time. Having a suspicion that she was related to me, I visited her, not as a relative, but as a Stanford student with a poem I had written and on which I wanted her opinion. So I had an excuse for visiting her. She read the poem and we discussed it. During the interview she was courteous, but very formal, as though she was wondering why I was really there. When I was ready to leave, I took courage and looked at her and said, 'Coolbrith isn't your real name is it. Your real name is Smith.' I really took her by surprise. She bolted upright in her chair, stiffened, and looked at me with daggers in her eyes. Then she softened and smiled.
>
> 'How did you know?' she asked. I told her of the understanding in our family that one of the family was a poetess living in San Francisco. Since Coolbrith was also a family ancestral name, I just put two and two together. I then expressed my curiosity about the secrecy. She told me that a long time ago her mother had made her pledge to keep her true identity a secret. The reason had been to avoid persecution and to aid William Pickett in his attempts to succeed in the practice of law.
>
> I told her that if she had made such a pledge,

that was good enough for me, and I would honor it. I then asked her how long I should honor it, and she said, 'That pledge is a sacred trust, and my mother died without releasing me from it. You must honor it as long as I live.'

Her final words to me were, 'When I die you can tell the world who I am. I am proud of my heritage.'

Ina's long and storied life came to a peaceful end on February 29, 1928, just ten days short of her eighty-seventh birthday. Deep regrets were expressed by many people, including academic and civic leaders and newspapers. In its tribute to Ina Coolbrith, the *San Francisco Chronicle* said, in part:

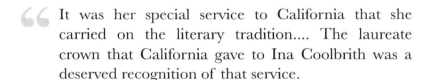

> It was her special service to California that she carried on the literary tradition.... The laureate crown that California gave to Ina Coolbrith was a deserved recognition of that service.

Ina had also prepared a third volume of her verse for publication, and Houghton Mifflin published *Wings of Sunset* posthumously.

At her funeral two men, strangers to one another, sat together on the same pew during the service. As the service ended, Henry Meade Bland, professor of English at San Jose Normal College introduced himself to Jesse Winter Smith. Bland introduced himself as a friend of Ina's, whereas Smith introduced himself as a relative. Bland seemed mildly surprised but appeared to give no thought to Smith's statement of family relationship.

Commenting on the close association he had had with Ina, Bland stated that he intended to write a story of her life. "I purposely did not crack a smile," Smith later reminisced, "and I thought to myself, 'You can't write her story. Why you don't even know her real name.'"

A New York City investigative newspaper reporter, Robert H. Davis, now entered the picture. Davis suspected Ina's true identity.

After Ina's funeral Davis sent a telegram to Professor Bland seeking confirmation of his deductions. Remembering that Jesse Winter Smith had introduced himself as a relative of Ina, Bland referred Davis to Smith. Davis then sent a telegram to Smith saying in part, "Rumor has it that Ina Coolbrith was related to the Mormon Prophet. Give us the facts."

"It was my pleasure," Smith reminisced, "to wire back, 'Ina Coolbrith was the daughter of Don Carlos Smith and the niece of Joseph Smith, the Mormon Prophet.'"

Jesse Winter Smith had kept Ina's secret for twenty-two years until her death, and now it fell to him to announce her identity to the world as she had suggested. Whenever the opportunity presented itself, Smith expressed his admiration and respect for Ina Coolbrith for her adherence to a principle of honor and for the pride in her heritage that she maintained throughout her long life.

~

References:

Ina Coolbrith's Scrapbooks at the Oakland (California) Public Library.

Ina Coolbrith Collections at the Bancroft Library in Berkeley, California, and the Huntington Library in San Marino, California.

Author's personal interviews with Jesse Winter Smith regarding Ina Coolbrith

JACK DEMPSEY BEGINS HIS BOXING CAREER

On June 24, 1895, Hyrum and Celia Dempsey became parents of a very special baby boy in the tiny LDS village of Manassa in Colorado's San Luis Valley. The parents named the boy William Harrison Dempsey. William was a born fighter, and at an early age he took on the nickname of "Jack" in honor of his hero, Jack Johnson, world heavyweight boxing champion at that time.

The Dempseys lived at the poverty level, and they moved frequently seeking work wherever it could be found. As a result, Jack spent little time in school beyond the elementary level, as his labors were needed to help support the family. Whenever he had some spare time he spent it in his favorite recreation, fighting, having learned the rudiments of boxing from an older brother.

Jack Dempsey's first professional fight occurred when he was only fifteen years old. Drifting into Montrose, Colorado, to visit some friends, he issued a challenge to Fred Woods, the 200 pound son of the local blacksmith. Fred was regarded as the toughest boy in town.

"We'll hire a place and make some dough," Jack claimed.

When Woods accepted the challenge, Jack hired a building known as the Moose Hall. With clothesline rope they outlined a boxing ring, and they spread sawdust for the floor of the ring.

On the night of the fight, Jack stood at the door of the hall collecting admissions, and when it appeared that everyone was there who was coming, he walked to the ring, took off his trousers, and hung them on a ring-post. Besides fighting, he was guarding the money in his pants pocket.

The fight, which was a real slugfest, went four rounds and ended with Woods unconscious on the floor. Grabbing a bucket of water, Jack doused Woods' face and revived him. Woods wanted to continue the fight, but Jack whispered to him, "The fight's over. They got enough for their money. You and me are partners." The two pugilists then shook hands, divided the forty-six dollars that Jack had taken in at the door, and went out together and celebrated.

Among the spectators that night was an experienced boxer named Andy Malloy. Approaching Dempsey at the end of the fight, Malloy suggested that they stage some fights with each other, and Jack readily agreed. They fought twice, once to a ten-round draw in Durango, and then back to Montrose and the same Moose Hall. Dempsey won the second fight in the third round, knocking out Malloy who was eleven years his senior.

Recognizing Jack's potential as a boxer, Andy Malloy became the first of several professional managers for Dempsey, and as they say: "the rest is history." On July 4, 1919, Dempsey became the world heavyweight champion by knocking out Jess Willard in the fourth round in Toledo, Ohio. He reigned as world champion until September 23, 1926, when he lost the first of two fights with Gene Tunney at Philadelphia. In the minds of many, Jack Dempsey was the greatest and most colorful heavy weight boxing champion the world has ever known.

~

References:

Ernest V. Heyn, *Twelve Sport Immortals* (New York: Bartholomew House, 1949).

Collier's Encyclopedia (New York: The Crowell-Collier Publishing Company, 1964).

OLD EPHRAIM WAS A BEAR TO REMEMBER

*O*ccasionally in the animal world, one animal of a species stands out as having superior, somewhat human-like, qualities. Old Ephraim, a huge grizzly bear, was such an animal. He lived in the early 1900s in the Cache National Forest east of Logan, Utah.

Measuring almost ten feet when standing, Old Ephraim weighed about 1,000 pounds. And he was smart. It took Frank Clark, part-owner of the Ward Clark Sheep Company, ten years to finally trap and destroy the huge beast.

Old Ephraim roamed the woods of the Cache National Forest, and like the other bears in that area, he feasted on sheep whenever he could. The bears were not content to kill just one sheep; instead they would attack a herd and fell as many sheep as they could. Then they would start eating the ones that were down. Rolling a sheep over on its back, a bear would rip open the flesh and eat the tender parts exposed. He would then leave the sheep to die a painful death. Almost every day Frank Clark would find one or two ravaged sheep, and he would shoot them to put them out of their misery. One day he found twenty-three such sheep.

Old Ephraim was an accomplished sheep eater. People knew when he had been around by the huge tracks he left. One of his tracks showed only three toes. But a sighting of Old Ephraim was a rare thing indeed. One day Sam Kemp, a friend of Frank Clark, suddenly found himself face to face with Old Ephraim. As the huge bear rose up to an erect position, Sam became so unnerved that he was unable to shoot his rifle. Fortunately, Sam and Ephraim parted company without incident, each going in opposite directions. On another occasion, Clark also saw Ephraim. The bear was carrying a sheep up the side of a mountain. Firing his rifle several times, Clark failed to hit the bear, but made him drop the sheep as he scampered out of sight.

Old Ephraim lived in a wallow, a large hollow in the ground that usually had water in the bottom. Old Ephraim apparently enjoyed a mud bath each morning before going out to forage for food.

On many occasions Clark would set a bear trap in Ephraim's wallow. But when returning to inspect the results, Clark would find that the trap had been moved up on the bank of the wallow without having been set off. This went on for ten years until one day when the trap sprang shut. Ephraim had not been caught, but the closed trap was again on the bank, and Ephraim had dug a new wallow below the old one. Clark knew that success was at hand. This time Clark set a larger trap and hid it in the mud. He also attached a heavy logging chain to the trap and wrapped the other end of the chain around a log about one foot in diameter and nine feet long.

Back at his camp, Clark was awakened by Old Ephraim's loud roars. The bear's right forefoot had been caught securely and painfully in the trap. The enraged bear made an attempt to run, but the log at the end of the chain quickly became caught in the trees. Then gnawing at the chain with his massive teeth, Ephraim managed to free it from the log, but only after breaking one of his huge teeth and bleeding profusely in the mouth and nose.

Ephraim knew where Clark was camped, and he headed in that direction, roaring with pain and rage. Clark was now awake, and with his .25-.35 rifle, he headed in the direction of the roaring. As the two foes came within sight of one another, Old Ephraim rose up to full height with the twenty-three pound trap still securely clamped on his uplifted right foot and the logging chain wrapped around his leg. Clark fired six steel balls into Ephraim's body, but the bear kept coming. With only one shot left, Clark thought it best to retreat and head for Logan, about twenty miles away, but he tripped and fell flat on his back. Clark's dog, Jennie, then took up the fight, and Ephraim began to swat at the dog. On his feet again, Clark took a chance, and at a distance of only six feet from the crazed bear, Clark sent his last shot into Ephraim's head. Ephraim fell, as his life came to an end.

Ephraim's body was too large for removal and the rocky mountain side would not permit a full burial, but Clark and others buried the animal as much as possible. They then piled branches and logs on top of the still exposed parts and burned them in an attempt at partial cremation.

Several days later, Dr. George R. Hill, then a scoutmaster of Troop 5 in Logan, heard of Ephraim's death, and he reported it to the Smithsonian Institute in Washington, D.C. Scientists at the Smithsonian doubted the existence of a grizzly bear in that part of Utah, and they requested his head, with an offer of $25.00 if the animal was truly a grizzly. Hill led his scouts to Ephraim's resting place, and they removed the head and shipped it to the Smithsonian.

They got their $25.00.

~

Reference:

Newell J. Crookston, *The Story of Old Ephraim* (Privately printed, 1959).

JOHN MORGAN: MISSIONARY SUPREME

J ohn Morgan's story begins with his early sojourn in Salt Lake City. He had been a Union soldier during the Civil War, and following the war, he attended college in Poughkeepsie, New York. After college he made a business trip to Salt Lake City, and liking what he saw there, he decided that Salt Lake City should become his permanent home. Thus, in 1866 at the age of twenty-three John Morgan, not a member of the Church, found himself living as a boarder in the home of Bishop Joseph L. Heywood, Bishop of the Seventeenth Ward.

One morning while having breakfast, Morgan told Sister Heywood of a strange dream he had just had. He was in Tennessee walking on a road going from Chattanooga to Rome, Georgia. It was a road he knew well for he had been on it as a Union soldier in the Civil War.

At one point, as he traveled in his dream, he came to a fork in the road, and there standing beneath a large tree was Brigham Young. Brigham told John Morgan that the right fork would take him to his destination at Rome, but if he (John) would take the

119

left fork he would encounter some priceless experiences that would give him a strong testimony of the divinity of the Book of Mormon.

"What do you think it means?" John asked Sister Heywood.

"I think it is a message from God," Sister Heywood replied.

Sister Heywood then expressed her feelings that at some time in the near future, John would join the Church and be sent on a mission to the Southern States.

"As a missionary," she continued, "you will find yourself on that road, and when you come to the fork you saw in your dream, remember what Brigham Young has just told you."

A year later, at the age of twenty-four, John Morgan joined the Church, and ten years later, as a missionary in the Southern States Mission, he found himself in northern Georgia walking along the road of his dream. Coming to a fork in the road he recognized it as the exact spot he had seen in his dream. The large tree was there just as he remembered, only that Brigham Young was not there under it. But Elder Morgan remembered what Brigham Young had told him in his dream. Although the right fork would lead directly to Morgan's intended destination, the missionary followed Brigham Young's counsel and took the left fork.

An hour's walk took Morgan to a beautiful valley which interestingly was named Heywood Valley. Twenty-three families made their home in that valley. Elder Morgan knocked at the first house he came to, and he was received with true southern hospitality. After an evening meal, he and his host talked religion for several hours. Elder Morgan explained the principles of the Plan of Salvation, and in doing so, he cited several Biblical scriptures. As the evening drew to a close, his host said. "I want to show you something." He then produced his own Bible, and showed Elder Morgan marked scriptures, the same that had been discussed that evening.

"A week ago a stranger came to my house and asked to see

my Bible. He then marked these scriptures and said that soon someone else would come and explain them to me." The scriptures marked by the stranger were the very scriptures Elder Morgan had discussed that evening.

During the next two weeks, Elder Morgan visited all the Heywood Valley families, and he found that several of them had also been visited by a stranger who had marked their Bibles. In the end, Elder Morgan taught and baptized twenty of the twenty-three families, and he organized a branch of the Church in that valley. The Methodist pastor was now the Branch President, and the Methodist Church building was now an LDS meeting house.

THIS STORY HAS A POSTSCRIPT. While staying in the home of his first convert, Elder Morgan wrote a pamphlet titled *The Plan of Salvation*. After finally arriving in Rome, he went to the Mosley Printing Shop and made arrangements for the pamphlet to be printed. When Mr. Mosley returned home that evening, he told his wife about the pamphlet and its author.

"He seems to be a perfect gentleman," he told her. "He is a very fine looking man and seems possessed of a most delightful personality."

"Did he try to convert you to be a Mormon?" she asked.

"No."

But the next day, after another visit from Elder Morgan, Mr. Mosley expressed that he was even more impressed with the pamphlet's author.

Mrs. Mosley's curiosity exerted itself, and she expressed a desire to meet Elder Morgan and judge him herself.

"Invite him to dinner," she suggested.

After dinner they visited amiably. The topic of religion was not brought up until the Mosley's turned the conversation in that direction. Elder Morgan took it from there, and at the end of a pleasant evening, the Mosleys requested baptism.

In subsequent years the Church published several tracts explaining various aspects of the Gospel. The pamphlet that Elder Morgan had written became the most popular of all the tracts published by the Church. Millions of copies have been printed and published throughout the world, and many baptisms have resulted. But the first baptisms attributed to the tract were those of the original printer and his wife, the Mosleys.

~

Reference:

Bryant S. Hinckley, *The Faith of Our Pioneer Fathers* (Salt Lake City: Deseret Book Company, 1956).

Made in the USA
Middletown, DE
08 September 2021